Tea in a Jam Jar

Birkenhead through the 1860s to 1959

Irene Kelly

*I`m dedicating this book to my children and
grandchildren with love and as proof we were all young
once upon a time*

Foreword

Irene, the author of this book and my younger sister, never fails to surprise me and when she told me she planned to write this book after researching our family ancestry, I was even more surprised than usual.

My earliest recollection of Irene was being told by my mum in 1941 when I was five years old that Irene then aged one, was not being evacuated with us to Welshpool- that lovely friendly Welsh town- as she was ill in Birkenhead Children's Hospital and couldn't travel.

On reflection we both experienced the Blitz and being bombed out (twice), the end of the Second World War, VE day, street parties and food rationing. We also experienced the rigours of a catholic education, teenage years dancing at the New Brighton Tower Ballroom, Elvis Presley, Bill Haley and the arrival of TV. The only thing we didn't share was National Service as girls were not conscripted.

All these events occurred during the 1940s and 1950s and I feel her recollections will help her children and grandchildren to understand how her forbears lived and survived in those years.

I also hope the book will give enjoyment to those people still surviving who lived in the 1930s, 1940s and 1950s and who will have their own special memories.

Eddie Kelly

Contents

Tea In A Jam Jar

Kildare – Monasterevin - Birkenhead

Who Are We Dad?

"Where were you born Dad?" "In Birkenhead pet,"
"Kelly is an Irish name isn`t it Dad?" "Yes pet my Mother and Grandfather were born there"
"Where Dad?"
"Don`t know pet."
"Where were you born Mum?" "Birkenhead love."
"Downey is an Irish name isn`t it Mum?"
"Yes love, your Granddads family came from Ireland"
"Where Mum?" "Don`t know love"
"Does that mean we are Irish Mum"
"Not altogether, my Mum`s name was Williams and that`s Welsh"
So there to the back of my mind to be buried for years was the Irish connection.

Way back in the fifties a good school friend Lily Cruise always spent her summer holidays on her Aunties farm in a place called Blessington, in County Wicklow. There she found me a pen pal, actually a boyfriend she was fed up with but Lily`s going to Ireland didn't make me think "Ireland! That's where my ancestors came from".

Years later when I decided to research my family I found that my blood was three quarters Irish, the rest a mixture of Welsh and Scottish.

In The Town Where I Was Born

Birkenhead is the town where I was born, where my great grandparents were married and brought up their families.

Birkenhead is made up of mainly English, Irish and Welsh, probably Irish being the greater number of people, the reason being that during the Irish Famine in the 1840's and onwards the Irish people had to move out of Ireland to survive.

One of the first stopping off places from Ireland was Liverpool. People who could not afford to travel further settled in Liverpool and as Birkenhead started to grow many moved over to Birkenhead.

Birkenhead for the most part was built by Irish labour. The houses, docks, railways and roads built mainly by Irish labour, it was the same picture throughout the world.

My genes are made up mostly of Irish with some Scottish and Welsh.

My four family names are Kelly, Mooney, Downey, and Williams.

I never knew either of my paternal grandparents, and only one of my maternal, my Nan whom I loved to bits. I will come back to my Mother's side later.

As I said I did not know my Father's parents. I wish I had. My grandmother died young and grandfather not too long before I was born. The family was poor as were most of the population. My Dad was born in 1907 one of nine children, sadly two of his older brothers died in the First World War, but I am happy to write that I remember all of the rest.

The Way They Were

The Kelly family was poor much the same as their friends and neighbours. The boys ran around barefooted, unemployment was high and so there wasn't the money to feed the family never mind shoe them. Dad told me tales of going around the market stealing anything they could eat. Stale bread sold at half price and the lady stallholder who didn't want the lads to get into trouble left all the old faded fruit for them to take but they were warned never ever touch the good stuff because "The Boys Reformatory is just up Laird Street"!.

Dad and his pals would go fishing in the docks and while they waited for a catch would strip off and swim in the buff, but would be chased off by the local bobby if he was in a bad mood, "What about a fishing rod Dad? I`d ask "Fishing rod" he`d say" a piece of string on a stick. We were all Huckleberry Finns in those days". They would spend hours on Seacombe beach looking for cockles and shrimps always after something for the table.

The girls weren't allowed to wander about like the lads. They had to stay close to home and their playing was always in the streets. Their brothers all had to look out for their sisters, Dad always said that girls were cherished and had to be treated with respect.

As the family got older and the bigger children found some work and a bit of money was starting to come in my grandmother opened a little shop off Watson Street selling fruit, veg and fish. She also bought a wheelbarrow for my Dad and his younger sister `Our Kit` to push around the streets selling the goods while Gran ran the shop. This would be around 1919.

As business got better a little horse and cart was bought so Dad could go further afield out into the countryside of the Wirral which at that time was very rural with lots of villages dotted about. It was nothing like the Wirral we know today. ""Our Kate had to stay and help in the shop and she wasn't very happy about that" Dad said.

Going to school was seen as more important for the boys than the girls, rightly or wrongly, the assumption being that girls would marry and stay at home which for the most part they did. The family lived in St Laurence`s Parish and the kids all attended the parish school. At a very early age Dad was told he had a heart murmur and was told he had to take care and Aunt Kit was told to look after him in school which she did very seriously. No one would pick on our George while she was about. She was two years younger but a little spitfire. Dad lived to the great age of ninety three and died in 2000. He outlived all of his siblings whom he missed very much.

Dad was a great reader and the teachers sat him for the eleven plus which he passed but was upset when he was told by his father that he couldn't go to grammar school, his reason being he wouldn't do for one what he couldn't do for them all. The fact that no one else had passed didn't change his mind. Dad said he would have accepted that they couldn't afford it as a better reason, so that later on when only one of his own children passed the exam for high school there was no way he wasn't going to let him go. So Dad left school at fourteen to work fulltime in his Mothers shop.

Lads in those days were allowed lots of freedom but girls, as I said, were kept very close to home. So while Dad was selling goods further afield around the Wirral, poor Kit was restricted to helping in the shop instead of travelling around with `Our Georgie` (Kit and George were very close for all of their lives). Dad carried on selling from the cart and Aunt Kit in the shop. When Dad was about seventeen things were going well and a little Ford car was bought. There were not too many about in the 1920`s so life must have been quite good, but over the next couple of years money was very tight as customers were so hard up they were unable to pay their bills. It was decided to close the shop and the family to look for work elsewhere.

We Get No Work So We Get No Pay

Getting work in those days was very hard. For the girls the choice was of factory work, shops, or going into service which meant living in your employer's home scrubbing and cleaning. This meant long hours and very little reward. For the lads it was shipyards, dockyards or signing up for the Merchant Navy. To get into the shipyards was difficult unless you had a relative or friend who could speak up for you. The dockyards were run on a very casual day to day basis. When a ship came into port the dock workers who had no work would hang around a place nicknamed 'The Pen' because it resembled a cattle pen and the men would be herded in just like cattle to see if they would be picked for a day or two's work. If you were lucky you had some money to feed your family until the ship sailed again and then back to the Pen.

In those days there was no such thing as benefits. If you had no work you had no pay. A man or woman had to go to the national assistance and beg for money to feed their families, but if they had anything to sell they were told to sell. If not they were given a pittance. There were Pawnshops on almost every corner and still a few when I was little.

Bon Voyage, Son

Dad decided to try his luck elsewhere, so he went to the shipping office in Liverpool and signed on to work his passage to Canada. Canada is a huge country and in the 1920's had a small population but was becoming very attractive to immigrants from all over Britain and Europe. Many people from England, Ireland, and Scotland settled in Canada, although many people from Wales went to South America and Argentina has a large Welsh community.

So Dad landed in Montreal with no money, completely on his own to find there was no work there either. Dad left Montreal and having no money the only way to get about Canada was to jump freight, which meant jumping on trains when no one was looking and hiding as best you could when the inspectors were searching. Thousands of men had to travel illegally to look for work and sometimes if caught you were thrown off at a town in the middle of nowhere and had to wait for the next train. This might be weeks away and if you couldn't find work or feed yourself you were arrested as a vagrant and made to earn your food doing whatever around the town to pay for a ticket on the next train. Dad said they only wanted to earn money to survive so there was no need for the police to arrest anybody but they did.

So Dad went off into the wilds of Canada looking for work, but the work outside of the cities was mainly farming and Dad knew very little about farming and any work he managed to get was by cheek and bluff. The farmers would ask if he could do a particular job and Dad would always reply "yes" yet he didn't have a clue what the job would be. His idea was to get the job and learn how to do it hopefully while doing it. One time he was asked if he could do 'Stooking', he had never heard of it but said yes he could, (which I think was collecting all the hay into bundles and tying it around the middle). Another time he was asked if he could handle horses and again he said "yes", but the only horse he had handled was the little mare at home and when he saw the huge workhorse the farmer used he nearly ran. Most of the time he got away with it which meant he was fed and had somewhere to sleep but I don't think much money crossed hands.

There was one farmer who seemed to take a shine to him and gave him a job. The farmer had a young daughter who was about fourteen who had never been off the farm, Dad said she must have been lonely for young company and was always talking to Dad asking him all about his travels and wanting to know if he had ever been to London "London!! I've never been more than fifteen miles from home and only a couple of miles to get on a boat to get here, London is harder to get to than here". After a few weeks the farmer asked Dad to move on as his daughter was getting too attached to him. Dad was upset by this because the girl was the same age as his sister Maggie at home and he felt the same about the girl as he felt about his younger sister. She was just a kid and lonely and Dad was only nineteen and feeling the same way too.

I think after that incident Dad realised he was homesick and Canada was not for him and after a bit more freight hopping he decided to come home. He did get as far as a place called Moose Jaw which is way up in the mountains towards North America.

Dad`s Return

Back home in Birkenhead his Mum was glad to have her son back in the fold. In those days if anybody left home to go abroad not many came back, not even for a visit.

Dad settled back into life at home with things no different than before he went away with not much work, very little money but just a little older.

Dad`s social life was always spent in the company of his brothers and sisters. He would have a pint with his brothers and if one of them had work, he would treat the ones out of work. It probably worked out well. There were three of them all good mates and after a pint they would collect their sister Kit and go off to the Penny Hop. Ted and Cissie were the oldest and I think maybe Cissie at this time might have been married or courting Jack McAllister. This would be in about 1927. Maggie and Albert would be young teenagers.

Girls didn't go into pubs when they were single and not very much after they were married either. It was World War Two that liberated women.

Shall we Dance?

It was now about 1928. Brothers and sister would go off to the Penny Hop where all the younger generation met to dance and usually meet their future partner. The Penny Hop was like today's dance club. Dad was a very good dancer and for the Waltz, Quickstep, Fox- Trot and Samba he was never short of a partner.

One of his partners whom he danced with mostly because she was a good dancer too, was to become Auntie May. May O`Brien married Uncle Joe, Dads older brother, and they carried on dancing while May and Joe were courting because Joe wasn`t a great dancer at that time and May preferred to dance with Dad. I think Uncle Joe improved his dancing to keep up with Auntie May.

The Penny Hops were all held in local halls mostly church halls and the Catholic Church hops were usually supervised by the priests and possibly the nuns from the local convent. They were there to make sure there was no Hanky Panky amongst the youngsters. The girls were particularly looked after because in those days to get pregnant outside of marriage was seen as awful and the poor girls would be looked down on. The couple would be forced to marry. This was known then as a shotgun wedding.

As to the girls who didn't get the offer of marriage some would be sent into homes for fallen women, which were dreadful places for young girls who had never been away from home. The babies would very often be adopted. Sometime a child would be brought up in the family as a sibling to their Mother and a child of the grandparents all to cover the shame felt by the whole family.

So it was at the Lauries Saturday night `Penny Hop` that Mum and Dad were to meet. They probably knew each other maybe not well as they only lived streets away from each other. Dad was seven years older than Mum but when you are a kid seven years is a lot when choosing your friends.

Now to Mum

William Williams married Jane Elizabeth Williams
1889c

Eleanor	*John*	*Susan Jane*
1890c	*1893c*	*1895*

My grandmother was one of three children. Of her father I know little about, but his name was William Williams and her Mother's first name was Jane, whose surname was possibly Williams too. Their children were Ellen, John and Susan my grandmother. Uncle John I remember as a big bruiser of a man and quite fond of a drink but a nice man, always happy to give me a couple of coppers for sweets. Nan's Mum liked a drink but Nan never liked the effect it had on some people so she never drank herself and I don't think Ellen did either. I don't know how her Dad died. Ellen (Aunt Nellie) and my Nan were close and Aunt Nellie's grandchildren were to be my friends as we grew up. They were the Millwards, Uncle Frank Auntie Nellie, Sally, Peggy, Frankie, Barbara and Peter.

The two sisters Nellie and Sue married two friends that had been in the army together Richard Downey and John Kennedy. Their brother John married a lady named Lena, I only remember her slightly but I remember their son Johnny Williams.

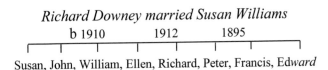

Richard Downey married Susan Williams
b 1910   1912   1895

Susan, John, William, Ellen, Richard, Peter, Francis, Edward

Nan in the old Birkenhead market

Nan married very young. It was 1913, she was only eighteen, it was possible she wanted to get away from a life of drudgery as was the case with so many women like her in those days . It was out of the frying pan into the fire. She married my granddad Richard Downey. I again know nothing of him only that Nan was to spend the next God knows how many years having babies nine of them, three girls six boys and one of the girls Josephine, was to die a baby.

As I remember Nan didn`t seem to have much but my memory is after granddad had died. There was no such thing as a widow`s pension and very little work about. It must have been hard going.

Anyway Nan was very young and I remember her telling me about her first effort at baking a pie and how she made the pastry without fat. After a lot of work at getting it to roll up and getting it onto the plate she cooked it and left it to cool while she went on a message. After telling her new husband not to touch it she came back found the pie which was as hard as a rock nailed to the wall. I don't know how she felt about it but if it had been me I would have been destroyed to have my first effort nailed to the wall and the filling running from it. Another time when she was waiting for her husband to come home from work via the pub she was worried there wouldn`t be much money left and while trying to keep the bit of dinner hot for him, she got angry and she picked up the plate, went to a pub in Market Street which had a door at both ends of the bar, she ran in one door slammed the dinner on the bar in front of him and ran out of the other door. She ran home and waited for him to come home not sure what to expect but I think he took it quite well. Nan was very brave I think.

Mum was born Susan Downey. As mentioned, she was the eldest of nine children, three girls and six boys but one of the girls died very young. I think that being the eldest girl was very hard. Having a Mum who must always have seemed to be pregnant, Mum said she didn`t remember a time when she, my Mum, didn't have a baby on her hip even as a very young child. She adored her Mother but I don't know how she felt about her Father as she never spoke about him. I wish I had asked more questions and shown more interest when she was alive.

Mum went to Holy Trinity Street School and when she went home she helped to look after her brothers and sister. There wasn't very much interest in education for girls who would only be getting married!! So the three Rs were seen as all they needed. But like Dad, Mum was to be deprived of her full potential. She loved to read and she was a wiz with figures and percentages all her life.

When she was fourteen she went into service but didn't live in because she was needed too much at home. She had to get up very early walk to work to scrub and clean. She worked for a family in Lorne Road, Oxton.   Oxton was where the very well to do of Birkenhead lived. Also the well to do of Liverpool moved to.

When Dad travelled around selling his fruit and veg in Oxton there was a toll bar across Shrewsbury Rd. You had to pay to enter, so it kept out the people considered unsuitable.

When Mum was about sixteen she got a job in a little café and while working there and going to the Penny Hop she met Dad. I think Mum was unhappy at home. Nan was still having babies and she must have wanted to move out of the crowded house. Her Mum encouraged her to move on. Dad was very unsure about getting married as they had no money and he had no work. But he knew Mum was unsettled at home so they got married in September 1932 in St Laurence`s Church. They lived in one room in the Eldon St area with one table, two little chairs, a bed and a few dishes. But

Mum was happy and never happier when cleaning her own home which was to stay with her all her life.

Mum was to stay very close to her family and losing her brother John the eldest lad was heartbreaking. He was in his thirties when he died of cancer and he died a very painful death, Nan and Mum nursed him and Dad washed him. John died about 1950. I remember it as a very unhappy time because Uncle John was a very well-liked man by friends and neighbours. He was very well known because he had a hand cart which he used to push around the streets singing out "any old rags" people would give him rags and jam jars and he would give the kids a goldfish in exchange. He was a very handsome man likened to Cary Grant. When he died he left a wife, a son and two daughters whom I am sorry to say I have had no contact with. John and Sheila are the only two I remember. Uncle Billy was to take over the handcart. He also became a well-known figure around town. His nickname was Dobby. Maybe he got the name because he pulled the cart like a horse, but I do remember he was always singing. We heard him before we saw him.

When Mum and Dad set up home, they stayed in the neighbourhood. They stayed very close to both families in the Parishes of St Laurence and Holy Trinity. Mum became good friends with Dad's family who by this time were a bit better off and had a nice home. She and Auntie Kit became very close friends for the rest of their lives.

Kitty married Fred Wiggins, Joe married May O'Brien, Ted married Maggie Rigny, Winifred (Sissie) married Jack McAllister, Albert married Annie Brannen and Maggie would marry Billy Wallace.

So this was to be the family circle, Kelly's, Downey's and the Wiggins a warm and happy circle to grow up in.

Aunt Mag's wedding to Billy Wallace. The first car I ever rode in was at this wedding and it would be a long time before I rode in another.

You Don't Know What You've Got Til Its Gone!
Put Up A Parking Lot!

Mum at this time was the only one married in her family. She was only eighteen and Dad was twenty five. The year is 1932. Mum and Dad were married and living close to both families in the Eldon St/ Market St, St Anne St areas, most of it gone now becoming car parks, a swimming pool, a train station and lots of factory units. This area was once the heart of Birkenhead, very heavily populated, throbbing with people and shops. The Streets mostly gone and now known as Conway Business Park, Europa Boulevard and the Pyramids shopping Arcade. Nothing left to remind us of the old town. There are a couple of pubs, two schools that are now council offices, a block of houses and two cinemas that are not used as cinemas any more. All our old play grounds have gone replaced by endless 'Carparks'!! You wouldn't recognise Conway St. The people who have left and come back, get lost and are saddened to see St Laurence's Church gone. This was the church where over half of the catholic population of downtown Birkenhead were married.

In 1934 my brother Georgie was born. In 1936 my brother Eddie was born and at the same time Granddad Downey died. He had been shot during World War One when he was fighting in Egypt and it had left him in bad health. Nan had her last child born just a day or two after he died. He was named Edward too. My two brothers then had an Uncle younger than them. Richie was born in February1938, and then me Irene, born in June 1940 at the beginning of World War Two.

Childhood! The Best Years Of Our Lives
1943-44

My first memory I think has to be being dressed by my Mum when I was probably about three or four. I can remember a mustard coat and leggings and a Bopeep hat all to match and being carried by my Dad into the book dept of Lewis's store in Liverpool. I remember the smell of the new books and the lovely colours. I know from future years that when we went to the Grotto it was a special day. We would all wear our Christmas clothes. There was very little money. Mum and Dad would have been saving all they could for this special day.

We would start the day taking the boat over to Liverpool to Lewis's to the Grotto to see Father Christmas and tell him what we wanted. Then we would go to the toy dept where we could choose a present. The lads would probably have chosen something sporty maybe a football, table tennis set or a game to while away the winter hours. I would go for books written by Enid Blyton always to be my top favourite. After we had chosen our presents it was upstairs to the café on the top floor for our dinner. Children today think nothing of going into a restaurant but to us this was special-only done once a year and we could choose anything, but fish and chips was favourite. Usually at home we would only have chips and maybe a few peas not because Mum and Dad were mean but there just wasn't any money for us all to have fish. I remember the lady in our `chippie` used to give the kids waiting in the queue a bag of batter bits; These were the bits that broke off the ends of the fish and the potato scollops. Delicious!

The Grotto

"Come here pet and I`ll pick you up
You're too little to stay on the floor
We are going to the grotto today
You were only little when we took you before"
I had on a brand new outfit
I can remember it to this day
Coat hat and leggings `in mustard`
Time to be on our way
Down to Hamilton Square Station
Soon we jumped on the train
Taking us to Lewis`s Grotto
`The biggest and best `, it says by the name
First we walked through the toyshop
The toys so bright and so new
Dad say`s for us to pick one
Pick something special for you
I don`t remember what was chosen
I wanted to wait for a while
My Mum she knew what I wanted
I knew she knew by her smile
So into the next door department
The smell I remember this day
The ink and the lovely new paper
All the books were there on display

15

"Take me to Enid Blyton
A Toytown book`s what I want
One about Noddy and Big ears
There`s such a lot to pick from"
Next we went to the Grotto
A spaceship is waiting there
To take us to see Father Christmas
Who sits in a big silver Chair
I held on tight to my Mum
As he sat with his great long white beard
I wanted to leave Santa's Grotto
I did not want to go near.
So again my Dad he did lift me
Took us up to the very top floor
To Lewis`s cafe he took us
A special treat was in store
"Pick what you want from the menu
HAVE WHAT YOU WANT FOR TODAY!!
Everybody had fish and chips, (A whole one)!!
Hope Dad`s got enough money to pay
We travelled home on the ferry
The water so cold and so deep
By the time we crossed over the Mersey
I think I fell fast asleep
Cos I don`t remember anymore.

Our Future Is Blown Up!

But other things had been going on before my memory kicked
in. There was a war going on of which I remember nothing.
I was born in 1940 in Beaufort Square which was blitzed and no
longer exists. I think with all the houses that were getting bombed
people were constantly on the move. Houses were blown up and if

people managed to get out alive they had to find places to live. As there wasn't any building work going on they had to squeeze into relatives or neighbours houses.

Whole families would live in one room and these houses were houses without hot water, the toilet was outside with no bathrooms and no electric. How did they wash themselves or do the laundry and where did they all sleep? On top of all this people were getting killed.

Husbands and sons called up to fight. Some men were exempt from the army usually old men and men with disabilities. Older men with children would have to work on the docks or in the shipyards. Single women started to do jobs that men had always done. They worked in ammunition factories drove buses, wagons, trains, and worked on farms. I suppose it was the one thing about the war that was good for women. They were never to be happy with being tied to the kitchen sink again, if they were lucky to survive the bombs.

Alongside all this was just trying to keep body and soul together and staying sane. So many people must have been close to breaking down. The noise of the siren going off to warn people of an air raid must have been the worst sound in the world. Dad said Mum was the fastest woman he knew to get four kids dressed and then run down with them to Hamilton Square underground station before the bombs dropped. There wouldn't have been many people hanging around after the siren went off.

Then you had to feed your families. Boats bringing in food from abroad were always at risk of being blown up so food was scarce. The Government decided to give people who wanted a plot of land, called `allotments`to grow their own vegetables, so Dad and Uncle Fred started to grow their own. Maybe this was the very first! "do it yourself " I'm not sure where Uncle Fred had his allotment but he and Dad always seemed to be together so I think they were not very far from each other. Dads plot was at the top end of Birkenhead Park-sometimes called `The top Park `

A big part of the park had been turned over to the home growers, so with their combined effort we never went short of any spuds or veggies. They also planted fruit if they managed to get hold of any seeds or plants. The fruit was typically English,-Gooseberries and Rhubarb- and maybe Strawberries, I remember dipping Rhubarb into sugar to sweeten it and then eating it like rock. We thought it was lovely. I tried it recently and it was foul but in those days it was good because there were very few sweets about.

Another thing we did, if we could get our hands on any cocoa, was to mix the cocoa with a bit of sugar in a bit of newspaper and lick it paper as well! Lovely! Cocoa came from abroad so it was very scarce.

I remember that Dad would tie a cushion around the crossbar of his bike, sit me on it and take me with him to the allotment "to help him," he said but I bet I was in the park playing more than helping him.

Rationing

In the war years pretty much everything was rationed and everybody had their own ration book which meant every time you went to the shops to the butchers, the bakers, the grocers, the dairy and the sweet shop you took your ration book with you. The man behind the counter would take the coupons, and give you your allowances, providing he had anything in the shop to sell. A cup of tea was a luxury then. Ration books would be around until 1952.

It must be very hard to imagine what it must have been like doing the shopping. You didn't queue at one shop you queued at half a dozen for maybe an hour or more. When the cry went up that a shop had food in you'd join the queue if you had any money to buy it. You might also be at the back of the queue and if the food supplies in the shop ran out, tough! An awful lot of fruitless time was spent in queues and to go home empty handed meant an empty table, but families and friends pulled together to survive.

Although I don't remember the war years I was growing up through them and the hardships went on long after peace was declared and a lot of what I am remembering happened up until I was twelve when rationing became a thing of the past.

Oh Baby it's Cold Outside!

The other hardship I remember was the cold in winter and cold is what it was. The winters were nothing like they are today. We would have thick snow which turned into thick ice and this thick solid ice which was great fun to play on would hang around until February and maybe March. This winter of 2010 has been like a blast from the past.

People can cope with the cold now because of wearing good clothes and having central heating in their homes. We had one coalfire to warm the flat.

The bigger kids would make sledges from any old wood they could find out of the bombed out houses and then make long slides on the thick ice. After a big push the sledges could really move. Everybody got to have a go on the slides, big kids, little kids, Mums and Dads, everybody was out watching or joining in and you could keep warm. The other thing I remember about the bitter cold was chilblains. This was caused by freezing feet and bad footwear. The cracked skin on the back of the heels was so painful and never really went until the spring no matter how much cream was rubbed in. 'Horrible'.

Rodney Street: Fearless and still wearing short pants

Now back to the rationing. Coal and coke were the only form of heating and I suppose the rationing for coal and coke came by way of being able to afford it and having to go and get it yourself. Up on the crossbar I would be again to go to the nearest coal depot that had any coal or coke in the yard. There would be long queues outside the yards. Dad would put his big coal sack under the chute, the coalman would pull a big lever and down would pour the coal into the sack, Dad would tie the top with string put the bag on the crossbar and sit me on the top and wheel the bike home again. When we got home Mum would go mad because my knickers would be black after sitting on the filthy coal sack, but come next time I would be back on the crossbar.

At this time we are in St Andrews Square. I think we had been re-housed after evacuation, because Beaufort Square had been bombed. It would be about 1942-43.

Once we got the coal home the fireplace in our flat would be stocked up to warm the place and at the side of the fire was a little oven. In which Mum used to cook. We had a gas cooker but we never wasted any heat from the little oven and there would always be something cooking maybe scones or potato cakes or a rice pudding depending on what was in the larder.

Nothing went to waste and any rubbish that could be burnt was burnt on this fire. At night all the vegetable peelings would be rolled tight in newspaper and put on the fire then covered in coal dust. Waste tealeaves would be poured all over to damp down the fire, the fire would burn slowly and in the morning a good poke of the fire would flare it up again. We would all wake up to a nice warm kitchen.

Getting out of bed on these freezing cold mornings and stepping onto icy floors can only be imagined by anyone who hasn`t done it. Nobody I knew had carpets only lino covering the floor boards. We walked on freezing cold lino with no slippers. Maybe we would have had our socks on in bed, but no warm nightwear and in our underclothes we would make a run for the warm kitchen where Mum would have our clothes getting warm on the fireguard.

We didn't have carpets but we did have a couple of Rag rugs which were homemade. Dad would get a flour sack from the Bakers; open the sides which then gave a good size for a rug. Then the sack would be boiled until spotless and get all the flour out. Any old woollen coats we could get would be cut into 3` by 1` strips and with a special needle the strips would be pulled through the sacking and back the other way until we had a very close woven and possibly a very colourful rag rug They were great to sit on in front of the lovely coal fire but they really got full of dust and were always getting beaten to get the dust out.

In bed we didn't` t have many blankets so to keep warm we four kids all slept in the same bed which was only a three quarter bed pushed against the wall with two chairs on the other side to stop us falling out. Dad would perch on the end and tell us stories. I think he made them up as he went along. I also think when I fell asleep he used to tell the lads ghost stories because the first chance our

Richie got he`d tell them to me to frighten me. I remember when I was put to bed on my own one night the lads had found a doll with eyes that rolled about so they poked out the eyes held a lit candle inside the dolls head and crawled along the floor with it. I think I was about five or six and never liked dolls after that so I never asked for one.

The Blitz

At this time children were being evacuated into the country for safety, away from the bombing which was very bad because of Merseyside being a huge docking area. Liverpool, Birkenhead and Manchester up the Mersey plus Cammell Lairds being one of the biggest shipbuilders in the country made us a prime target for the Luftwaffe (The German Air Force).

Just before one bad air raid Dad and Uncle Fred were having a pint in a pub called `The Duke `on their way to work on the night shift at the docks when the sirens went off. This was the signal for everybody to go underground but these two invincibles decided they wanted to finish their pints so the landlord threw the pub keys at them telling them, telling them to lock up on their way out. What a Mistake! What people would leave these two in charge of an empty pub, which must have been mannah from heaven to Dad and Uncle Fred so God knows what they must have been like after the air raid. Mind you there wasn't that much beer and spirits about during the war, but there would have been less in that pub next morning.

All the cities and towns, which were the target of the Germans, had suffered nights upon nights of blitzes and as you can imagine were very dangerous places to have to live in. Many people where blown up where they lived, worked or on the way to the air raid shelters. Many people were buried alive and the bombed out remains could fall down at any time. Anyone who tried to salvage anything from their homes could have the house fall down on them. I was born in 1940 and have no memory of this time but I remember I grew up on the tales being told.

Well Lane Tranmere

No school today!!! The school has been blown away

Evacuation

It was decided at this time by the Government to evacuate all the children from all the places that the Germans were bombing and to send them to safe places in the countryside. All the kids were rounded up, name tagged and taken to the Railway Stations to be sent to homes of people they didn't know, and in many cases to people who didn't want them but had no choice about taking them. It was all part of the war effort.

Some parents refused to let their children go, but if the alternative was a chance your children could be killed most parents sent them off. The parents found themselves between the devil and the deep blue sea.

Lots of these children had very miserable times away from home, very homesick missing their parents, brothers and sisters. There was never a lot of effort put into keeping siblings together. If you were lucky you might have relatives living in the countryside and they might take you, but you might end up as a workhorse for maybe someone not very nice.

Lots of the kids were sent overseas to Australia and America in which you had to travel by boat over the Atlantic and if you were going to Australia it was much further. This was very dangerous because the German subs were sinking ships all the time and it was said ships carrying evacuees were sunk and hundreds of kids died.

Dad and Mum decided they didn't want their kids to go off to strangers and an unknown place as most kids had to. They packed a few bits and took the three lads and went off to Wales on the early morning milk train and ended up in a place named Welshpool, about seventy miles away from Birkenhead on the English Welsh border.

It wasn't an easy trip and took most of the day getting on and off trains looking for somewhere to stay and finally Dad walked into a pub named 'The Mermaid Arms' in Welshpool and asked the landlord did he know of anywhere they could put up for the night. When he heard they were from war torn Birkenhead he told them to go along the passage (The Mermaid Passage) and see his missus who would help and she did. She told Dad she had one bedroom and two beds but no room for Dad, but Dad had to go back the next day to be at work so he slept on a chair in the saloon bar.

The next day Dad had to go back leaving his wife and three sons in the care of this lovely man and wife who had told him not to worry as they would take care of them. The reason I wasn`t there was because I had pneumonia and was in the Children`s Hospital seemingly very ill.

The next morning the lads woke up in paradise.

The landlord`s wife found a cottage for Mum to move into and a collection of furniture to fill the rooms. The people of Welshpool really took the war torn exiles to their hearts and the lads had never had so much freedom. Welshpool at that time was a small country farming town very quiet and the only traffic would have been from a few motors and horse drawn carts and farming equipment. Petrol was rationed so there were not many cars about, but not many people owned cars in those days.

The lads at that time would have been aged, Ritchie two, Eddie four and Georgie six. Eddie and Georgie got up that first morning and went exploring and found fields, cows, sheep, and poultry. Never had they seen anything like it, trees to climb, a river, and a canal to play in.

There were little passages with strange names like Mermaid Passage and Bear Passage, odd names for a country farming town. It's hard to imagine what it must have been like for the boys who only knew bombed out buildings and were too young to have been allowed out to play because of the wreckage on the streets in Birkenhead.

The lads settled in very well, but Mum was lonely and missing everybody back home, worrying how safe they all were. So you can imagine how happy she was when Dad came down for one visit and with him came the Wiggins family, Auntie Kit, Uncle Fred, Freddie, Peggie, Mike and Franny. This would have been the icing on the cake to Mum if the baby (myself) had been with them but now she had Kit with her she was happier.

Dad and Uncle Fred spent what time they could with their families but had to go back for work promising to look after the baby in hospital and be back soon. So now there were seven kids and Mum and Aunt Kit in one small cottage. God knows where they all slept but it wouldn`t have worried them as long as the kid's were safe.

Now all the cousins were together it gave Richie more freedom because Peggy and Freddie were old enough to keep their eyes on the youngest two- Richie and Franny. These two were very good pals and a couple of tearaways.

So now they could really enjoy themselves and be more adventurous and one day while playing in the canal (I don`t think they could all swim if any of them could) Eddie tripped over his shoelace and fell into the canal and was drowning. He went down three times and a passing soldier home on leave dived into the canal and saved him.

The kids were to have many good times in Welshpool and I don`t remember any of them saying a bad word about their evacuation.

I was finally taken out of the Children`s Hospital because it was bombed. I don`t know if anyone was hurt but the children who had to stay in hospital were transferred to Hoylake Cottage Hospital, me included.

But Dad decided I would be safer in Welshpool so he took me out and he and Uncle Fred took me onto the train to join the others making Mum very happy. Mum told me Aunt Kit was waiting with a big shawl around her shoulders, opened her arms and wrapped me in next to her bosom and that became my new hospital bed. I was very close to Aunt Kit, in my childhood there are so many things I can remember that included Auntie Kit, Uncle Fred, and our cousins which will show as I go on.

As the war progressed and the bombing stopped, it was decided to go back home. Dad took a last walk through the village and ended in the grounds of Powys Castle the home of the local gentry and while trespassing (which he didn't know he was doing he said!) he was stopped by the lady of the house asked who he was and when she found he was one of the fathers of the evacuee children she invited him in, gave him something to eat and showed him around the estate. When he was leaving she gave him a food parcel to take home and said the village would miss the children very much..

So the goodbyes were said and I think the kids must have been unhappy to leave but Mum and Auntie Kit were glad to go back home and see their friends and families.

A very old pub in Welshpool I'm sure Dad and Uncle Fred paid a visit to

The next two pictures are of `The Mermaid Pub' and Mermaid passage the first port of call where Dad got help from the landlord, now sadly closed down and `Bear Passage' which led to the cottages where we lived for the duration of our evacuation.

I wish I could remember

Out on the Milk train everyone but me
Looking for safety away from the sea
My Father decided to go into Wales
To find us a cottage away in the dales
He settled on Welshpool, a small country town
He asked a pub owner, would he ask around
"Go up the passage and look for the wife
She`ll give your family a bed for the night"
No room for Dad he had to sleep rough
He`s not very big but really quite tough

The very next day a cottage was found
Not like at home were our flat was bombed down
The lovely people gave what they could
A chair, a table, for the fire lots of wood
Mum made it cosy or so I've been told
Something to eat and keep out the cold
Poor Dad set out, he had to be back
Back on the docks which were under attack
Don't worry Sue I`ll be here next weekend
The little one with me if she`s on the mend

True to his word the very next week
Popped in his head to have a peek
"I haven`t the little one! But what about this"
In walked Auntie Kit and Uncle Fred
Our cousins by the hand were led
"Hi Kit" says Mum "Are you here for the day?"
"No, if you`ll have us we're here to stay"
So this is it!! How it should be,
Everyone together, except the baby.

The lads were in heaven, lots of places to play,
The river, the canal, they were in every day.
I was told of our Eddie who nearly drowned
The soldier who put him back on dry ground
There were fields, there were horses,
There were cows, there were sheep
They only went home when it was time for sleep
Out went the kids, everything to see
The river, canal, were pure ecstasy
The trees full of apples there to be picked
Till your stomach ached
And you made yourself sick.

Another week later out on the train,
Dad and the little one, out they came.
Into auntie Kitties welcoming arms,
"Into my shawl she`ll come to no harm"
I wished I could remember
The places they had seen
All lovely memories
Of days that had been.

So many years later the little one a Nan
By chance I was in Welshpool, buying a van
I walked down the high street
Found each little spot
The places so vivid
I walked through the lot

My wish to have been there came true that day.
I really shared in their fantastic stay
The town the same as in stories told
Became mine, mine to enfold.

Back Home
1942-43

Back home our flat in Beautford Square was gone, blown up, so
we had to move in with one of Dad`s family in St Anne street. I
know at one time they had lived in Nan`s front room for a while
until Beautford Square, then we were evacuated. Dad didn't like
living with Mum`s Dad. I don`t think they got on because
Granddad tried to treat Mum like a child telling her what to do. If
she was having a natter on the step with a neighbour he would tell
her to get in and if she went out, what time to be in. It must have
been hard for Mum to go back after leaving to get married.

Families moved in with each other all the time losing their
homes in the bombing or short of money and not able to pay their
way. But the one thing the war was to give was more jobs and a bit
more money.

So back from Welshpool into very crowded conditions the
council finally gave us the keys to a flat in St Andrews Square the
place where my memory starts. Around this time Auntie Kit moved
in just two verandas away from us. We lived in twenty-one, the
Wiggins in thirty seven and the Millwards two balcony's up five

flats along. At about the same time Nan moved into another block of flats called Vernon Place, both blocks in Conway Street very close together.

The two blocks of flats have now gone to make way for the flyover built in the sixties as part of the redevelopment of Birkenhead and tunnel access.

The flyovers gone now to make way for a Market and shops, so when you shop in Wilkinsons you are treading on my old homestead. There was also a church next door to our flats called St Andrews which I will come back to. Vernon place is now a small Chinese village. St Andrews Square is replaced by the big store Wilkinson's, and the Mecca Bingo, Oh and a carpark!!

As I said St Andrews Square is where my memories start and as well as I remember the Grotto I also remember VE day, ` Victory in Europe` the end of the war in Europe. However this was not the end of the war in the Far East. That part of the war was to carry on for some months but the threat of Hitler invading England was over and the soldiers could start to come home and the celebrations started.

Celebrations

With the end of the war declared, the people hit the streets and there was cheering, hugging, singing and dancing and crying for the men still away, the people who had been killed and disabled, and for the children orphaned. Happy days, but so sad.

He party atmosphere was to last for days and days and people were dressing the children in all sorts of patriotic outfits. There were Union Jacks everywhere. Auntie Kit who was a marvel with a sewing needle made me a white skirt with a bib front and on the bib had sewn a flag. What I remember is being carried by Dad on his shoulder and when he got tired I was passed onto an uncle. I was about four at this time and the youngest child in our two families so

I was well looked after. Everywhere I went in my little outfit people put coppers in my hand and it seemed a ton of money to me.

So down to Hamilton Square everybody went where bands were playing and the dancing and singing went on, and the town dignitaries made speeches. I watched it all from somebody's shoulders as did all the kids and we all waved our flags at each other.

It meant shame for the Japanese to surrender so that war carried on until the Americans dropped two nuclear bombs on Japan, causing untold death and destruction to the country.

The parties were being organised and Auntie Kit who was good at sorting things became the main organiser for St Andrews Square. She started collections for money and every Friday night up until the day of the parties, which were to be throughout the British Isles, coppers were collected to pay for the food. The women did without their sugar, butter and dried fruit rations for all the cakes, pies and scones that would be baked.

There would also be a party queen; she would be the one who collected the most money. So the older kids went out asking people for a penny for the queen, a bit like asking the lads asking for a penny for the guy around Bonfire night.

The decorations started to go up around the verandahs that circled the flats. Red, white and blue bunting was hung outside every flat hanging over the balconies. Some of the neighbours even painted the bricks red, white and blue too.

The trestle tables and bench seats were borrowed from Thompson's Mission, I think. Sheets off the beds were bleached white and made do as tablecloths. There were jellies, fairy cakes and sandwiches. My job had been to stick two crackers together with icing and jam. They must have been the original `jammy dodgers`. We had pop and orange, no coke!! It hadn't reached here yet but it was certainly in America. I think the grown-ups probably made do with salad and let the kids have the goodies.

The entertainment was a piano, an accordion, mouth organ and always a man playing the spoons. There was always a pianist at any party anywhere and there would be singing and dancing and everybody joined in. Older neighbours were carried if they couldn`t walk. Nobody was left out and then the crowning of the party queen with her silver handmade crown.

This all happened when I was about four or five and it would all be repeated about 1948 at the time of the Festival of Britain, which was arranged in London as a celebration of the war being over. All the soldiers back from the Far East and the prisoners released from the dreadful camps the Japanese had held them in were there. I think the party I remember is a mixture of the two.

Being eight I was old enough to collect money for the 1948 party and again Auntie Kit organised it and there was more time to get money together. It was decided that there would be a party queen and a princess, and again the two who collected most would be crowned. The queen and princess were Violet Stewart and Muriel Ives and they were dressed in lovely long white dresses and little white hair ribbons. They sat on decorated chairs.

Local photographers were travelling around taking pictures of all the street parties and took a picture of little Kenny Ives, who's birthday it was that day and Auntie Kit had made him a little cake which I was giving to him. I also had a pretty white dress as there was no way Auntie Kit would see me left out. Weeks later the Claughton cinema, now gone, was showing all the pictures of the street parties. The cinema was full with everybody wanting to see their party up on the big screen like film stars. There was Violet and Muriel queen and princess being crowned and then the next photo was little Kenny Ives with his cake and me giving it to him. They had decided to show it because Kenny's Dad had died when Kenny was a baby, which was sad but a lovely thought and one that made us film stars for a day. Oh fame!!!.

As I said the two parties run into one so if anybody notices any time warps I am sorry.

'Don't go to Thompsons you only get a Bun tell Mrs Thompson to stick it up her…!' are some of the not so very nice words of the song we sang after eating the buns given to us by the kind Thompsons.

Thompsons Mission where the tables were borrowed from for street parties is one of the places left that has never changed. It looks exactly the same today as it did when we were kids and it is still doing good works and looking after the needy.

When we went to Thompsons we went to see the magic lantern show and to get a free bun. The lantern looked like its name and it had five glass sides. Pictures were slotted behind the glass. There was a big sheet hung on the wall at the back of the stage. Miss Thompson would tell us a story from the bible. Someone would turn the lantern round and round and the bible pictures would light up on the sheet and appear to move. This was our magic Lantern. Then we would queue up for the bun.

In the summer, days out were arranged to Helsby hills or Talacre?. The older lads could go on a camping holiday for a whole week to Wales. Our Georgie went once.

Health And Safety! Forget It

It`s 1944 and the war is over in England and life begins to get back to some kind of order but we are surrounded by the bombed out buildings, which was a kind of paradise playground for kids to play in but a nightmare for parents trying to keep their kids safe. The lads who thought playing in a building were the roof could fall in at any time was great and never gave a thought to the danger. The church next door as I have said was St Andrews. The back end of the church had been bombed. It was still used at the front and we went to Sunday school there each week but we had to go in the front door because there was a big gaping hole at the back where someone had nailed a few planks of wood over the hole to stop us falling out. But it didn't take the lads long to pull the planks off and start to play daredevil games such as jumping from the first floor to the ground which was covered in all sorts of bombed debris. Another time I was playing by the church wall and the lads on the other side were larking about throwing bricks over it. They were going to build something with them and one came over hit me on the side of the head. I was pouring blood and my Mum had to run me up Conway St to the General hospital. There was no cars, no taxi's just shank's pony. Don't believe me? I`ve still got the scars. To catch the blood she held a pair of her knickers to my head, long legged ones and when I said "Not your knickers Mum" She replied "Stop moaning if you hadn`t got in the way of the brick I wouldn't be running to the Hospital ruining my knickers". No molly coddling there then!

At the side of the church was a Cemetery with old gravestones, flat ones, tall ones, and some table shaped. We would go in there to play and while the lads were jumping out of the bombed out church we were playing very genteel games on the gravestones. House or hospital seemed to be our favourites. On the flat tombstones we would lay on for a bed and on the table shaped we would lay old newspapers for a table cloth and get out our little dolls teaset and lay the table. We would sit there daintily sipping cold water out of little cups and when it was time for bed lay down on the flat graves, while all around us lads were jumping out of glassless windows or playing Cowboys and Injuns, running past us holding one of their hands out in front as the reins and smacking their backside for the rump of the horse shouting `Gee up Trigger`. All the horses were called Trigger after Roy Rogers `s horse which was the kids favourite at the Mickeypops club on Saturday morning. After a while we would get fed up with our posh little cups and go and play cowboys and Indians with the lads.

St Andrew`s Square and St Andrew`s church

I am just too young to remember
When the bombs they came falling down
But what is stuck in my memory
Are the buildings in heaps as they lay on the ground
We had no green fields to play in
Our playground was covered in bricks
And the beams that held the roof on safely
Had been blown into very fine sticks
There was no such thing as health and safety
We played in places not fit
We played in the front of St Andrews
Cos the back had had a direct hit
The roof was wide open to heaven
You could see the stars and the sun
We never thought of the danger
We only enjoyed all the fun
"We don`t want you playing in St Andrew`s
Make sure you do what we say"
We couldn`t find anywhere more exciting

Nowhere better to play
So we scrambled into the church yard
The average age about eight
We couldn`t walk in properly
Cos the bobby had locked the back gate
"And do you know why I lock it
It's to keep you bloody kids out
You know you shouldn`t be in there
And sent us home with a clout"

The Mickeypops

A Four Legged Friend
A Four Legged Friend
He`ll Never Let You Down
He`s Honest and Faithful Right Up to the End
My Wonderful One, Two, Three, Four Legged Friend

The Mickeypops club was on Saturday mornings at the Savoy Cinema. Kids only and there we saw all our idols, Roy Rogers and his trusty steed Trigger.

There wasn`t any trick Trigger couldn`t do and he saved somebody`s life every week. Roy also had a side kick, Gabby Hayes, he was the cook. Roy always sang a song, usually about trigger and we all joined in.

Wild Bill Hickock had a trusty steed too but he couldn`t do tricks as good as Trigger. There was also `The Lone Ranger`, and his trusty companion was Tonto, an Injun who was on our side. But Roy was our favourite. He was always fighting the savage Injuns who attacked our wagon trains and nearly got the better of us. But then, what always lifted the roof and had about three hundred kids cheering in the cinema was at the end of the film when the cowboys were down to the last men. We would hear the bugle blowing and in would race the cavalry usually with our hero in front who had gone off on his own to find them. Hurrah!! Roy and Trigger saved us again.

Other favourites of us all were Laurel and Hardy who had us falling about laughing. Abbot and Costello were just as daft.

I also went to the `flicks`, a nickname for the cinema, with my Mum and Dad though they never went together because they liked different films. Dad liked action films, but Mum liked the romances so over the years I must have seen most of them. I was brought up on make believe as we all were. The Hollywood films were the best, with huge stars, the obvious John Wayne Dads favourite. Mums favourite was Cary Grant. There were hundreds of them and everybody queued up to see them, long lines of people waiting to see their idols. We loved them all.

I remember the old Queens cinema had a sign 'CHILDREN IN ARMS FREE'. I must have been about five and Mum was still picking me up to carry me in to avoid paying for me and she would stagger under the weight. The doorman who knew all his regulars used to say "Now Come on Sue, your pushing your luck" Mum would point to the sign, he would laugh and she would get away with it for another week. The only one not laughing was me. Imagine the shame of still being carried in by your Mum. She never carried me out that I remember. The poor old Queens was closed down because the `Posher` cinemas had upholstered seats and the Queens still had benches and when too many people pushed on one end somebody used to fall off the other. It was hilarious to the kids but the adults wanted better. After that it became a dance hall then a club. It was pulled down and replaced by the Market and another- Yes! that`s right another car park.

Cinema was just about the biggest form of entertainment for everybody. Television was still a few years away. Even waiting in the queue was exciting while you were waiting to go in. Buskers would sing for any Coppers that could be spared and you would always see your school friends waiting as well. When you got nearer any of the doors at the side of the cinema (which were the emergency exits) one of the kids already inside would open the doors and we would sneak in without paying. But we didn`t kid anyone because the staff inside knew all the tricks. They had probably done it all themselves and now were paid to keep out anyone who sneaked in. They gave us a clip around the ear and threw us out. The odds were they knew your Mum and Dad so you hoped they wouldn't tell.

There were also other characters about to keep us amused and the one I remember was little Jimmy Kelly,(I don't think he was related but maybe he was) who would be outside the Ritz cinema which had a huge frontage of glass doors. Jimmy would go to one of the doors and pull faces at the commissionaire who stood there decked out in his finery like a navy admiral. He would run at Jimmy who would run to another door pulling his face again. This would go on for a while until Jimmy got fed up and go off to torment the man at the Chippy, (chip shop). Jimmy was autistic, most people looked out for him and he was a happy soul.

The Ritz cinema was a beautiful Art Deco building that also put on stage shows. Cliff Richards played there with the Shadows as did lots of big names of the day. The Ritz Cinema has now of course gone for a 'you know what'

Night and day.
Now you can only see carparks!

40

School

When it was time for me to go to school in 1944, I wanted to go to the same school as my best pal Josie Owens so that is where I went. That was St John`s School in Oliver St. It was a Church of England school. I settled in very well I think. Very happy to be with the kids I played with at home Josie, Norma Nugent, Anne Birch, Betty Billington and of course, Peggy and Barbara Millward our cousins.

St John`s School and St John`s Church were also pulled down to make way for the Pyramids. Probably the only bits of Grange Road left recognisable are Charing Cross and Woollies, but I will say it was always exciting to go down Grange Road on a Saturday because you met everybody there. It was the hub of the Town. Now back to school.

I was to find out after six weeks my friends had all been christened Protestants and I was a Catholic so the Catholic Church wanted me in St Werburghs. In those days you went to the school of your religion. So out I was taken crying and into St Werburghs where I knew nobody.

The boys had their own school in Grange Road so I couldn`t go to them for a cheer up. I hated this new school because I missed my friends and all the other kids had already made friends being there six weeks before me so I don't think I made a very good impression. I remember having to stand in the corner until I stopped crying and the teacher hitting me on the back of the legs with her ruler. I was four! I must have settled down at some point but I do know I didn`t like school much after that. This was about 1944 and the war was still on.

The school I went to although named St Werburgh`s was based in St Laurence`s School because our school had been bombed and we were allocated two classrooms in St Laurence`s infants, three

41

classrooms in St Laurence`s Middle school, and two classrooms in Conway St senior girls School with two half days use of the gym.

We shared the playground but we had to keep to our own end. Looking back it was a bit ridiculous as we weren`t supposed to mix at school but when we went home we all played together as friends, crackers!! but we had to obey. I don`t know who`s rules they were but my guess would be they were of the Church which still kept a tight watch on their parishioners in schools and churches. When we went home we were never kept apart as we were all friends and neighbours and we were all looking out for each other.

So off I went to the St Laurences, over Conway St across Eldon St down any little side street that led onto Park St, but in the summer if I had a penny I would go past the Dairy to get a homemade ice cream.

We learnt to read and write and do arithmetic known as the three R`s-reading, 'riting and 'rithmetic. Later when we were eight we moved upstairs. Because our facilities were basic our education was limited. We read History and Geography, but not for us, the luxury of labs and craft rooms. We learnt all we knew from books. But we didn`t know any different. We never knew other schools had these facilities.

I remember the dark little passageway that led into the school buildings and the very first class I went into was across a tiny playground for the tots. This playground led into another passage, past Middle School buildings and onto a huge playground or so it seemed to us little ones. We weren`t allowed past our own tiny area until we were eight when we went upstairs to the Middle School classrooms and then onto the big kids playground which I remember with awe passing through all the buildings which were St Laurences.

We never saw the inside of the school because we were confined to our own little sections. When I left the Middle School to go to Conway St a new School was built for St Werburgh`s in Whetstone Lane just too late for our class.

My very first teacher was Miss Stredder who put me in the corner for crying on the first day I went there from St John`s School. I also remember how she always compared me to our Eddie who was the clever one and I suppose our Richie must have had the same treatment,. Maybe she thought I was a whiner because I cried a lot and she liked to have a go at me but I do know I was glad when I was moved. I don`t remember any other infant teacher so maybe I was with her until I went upstairs.

I found out years later that I was somehow related to her, that she lived very close to the flats on Conway street so that`s how she must have known how the lads fared at the boys School.

Now it`s 1948 and I`m eight and going upstairs feeling quite scared going into the class where Miss Smythe is the new teacher and totally different to Miss Stredder as she seemed to like the girls. Miss Smyth as well as teaching all the usual subjects introduced us to needlework and painting which I wasn`t any good at but I was quite good at sewing.

At this time I was quite a good reader because I was really into Enid Blyton. I always spent my pocket money from when I was tiny on Toy Town comics and the adventures of Noddy and Big Ears and then moving on later to the Tales of the Five and the Secret Seven. It was wonderful years later to buy the same books for my own children and smelling the ink in the new books took me back to my childhood. Memories!!

After Miss Smythe we were taught by Miss Tweedale` Smith whom we thought was posh because she had a double barrelled name. We had never met a person with two surnames before but how useful it would have been years later when researching my ancestors if everybody had held on to their Mothers surname as well as their Fathers.

Throughout school we only ever had one Headmistress- Miss McBennett. She was a lovely teacher who sometimes took over the lessons. She sat at the Teachers desk and sometimes would forget to keep her knees together. She wore the longest legged bloomers in the world right down to her knees and we would sit and giggle as though we had never seen them before but all our Mothers and Grandmothers wore them. They even hung them on the washing lines which hung over the verandas for the world to see and also wrapped them around your head and took you to the Hospital. They were nicknamed Passion Killers but didn't live up to that name because people still had big families.

The schools in those days were very strict and you were punished with the cane, (girls and boys alike). Once you entered Middle School at eight years old you were old enough to be punished. Previously the ruler was used. I remember on many occasions holding my hand out for the dreaded six of the best.

My trouble was not being naughty but playing the fool which I did quite often. One time I was sent to Miss McBennett for my punishment and she said to me "Irene why do you have to keep entertaining the class and having to come to me. You know, it hurts me more than it hurts you having to give you the cane" Well I don't know how bad her pain was but if it was worse than mine well I'm sorry! But she really didn't like giving the cane because her hand would hover until she had the courage to hit you with it and I'm sure she closed her eyes as she did. Not like Miss Coffey who would cane you without a thought and when you went home you didn't complain, you said nothing because your parents would say "You must have deserved it" and would keep you in the house as another punishment and if you tried to argue your case they would add another day.

I have to say that Mum and Dad never raised their hands to us but Mum would threaten us with Dad, "Wait till your Father gets home. You'll be sorry". We knew smaller things she would forget but anything serious Dad would be told and Dad had the gift of the LOOK and that look spoke volumes, I don't remember the punishments but I do remember the LOOK. There was another way he could terrify you just by standing up and starting to unbuckle his belt and you knew you had to disappear before the belt came off but I can honestly say that belt never came off.

I remember one time sitting on the arm of his chair and the word bloody slipped out. He slowly turned around gave me the 'Look' and said "you have ten seconds to get out of my sight", and started to unbuckle his belt. I shot out of the flat over to Auntie Kits. She knew Dad would never hit me, but she told me off for swearing which was an absolute taboo with Dad. I would always run over to Auntie Kits where her Welshpool arms were ever waiting. Our Eddie also remembers a lecture he received for swearing and he was grown up. We never heard Dad swear in front of women or children. However when he was decorating in the house he was always in a foul mood, so a few mild curses would slip out. We would all run a mile to get out of his way.

Back to school my best friends all through school were Anna Moody, Beryl Nolan, Brenda Pickstock and Cathy O`Donnell.

We went through school together from when we were five until we were fifteen and left school. The only one I saw regularly after was Brenda. We started at the Co-op together at different Branches. I left she stayed.

There were two regular visitors at the school. One was the priest, the other the welfare nurse and her job was to check for sores and head lice. What she would do, would be to stand behind the black board and we would one by one join her and have our hair checked and if she found any lice she would give you a card to go to the clinic. There you would be shorn very short and doused in something very smelly and foul. I think it was a concoction of paraffin and carbolic soap and if she found any sores you were painted in a purple ointment. It was quite common to see bald-headed purple spotted kids playing out. I am happy to say I never had to go through it but that was because mum was a fanatic at keeping us clean and every other Friday night was Zuleo night. You have to remember this is all happening in the aftermath of war and sanitary conditions were very hard to maintain. There were lots of solutions to helping us keep clean.

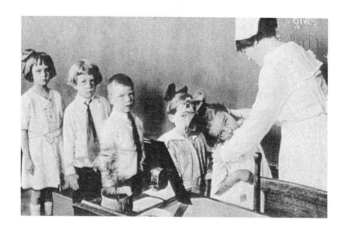

Friday Night Is Zuleo Night

Friday night I`m playing a game
All of a sudden I hear my name
The sound of her voice
It's my fortnightly fright
"I---reen, zuleo"
"Ah aye mum not tonight"
"Get in here you don`t want nits
I`ve got to give your head a blitz"
On with the oil
My hair it lay flat
On for twenty four hours
I hated that
Back out to play
I don`t want to go
"You are in my way
So off you go"

Hiding my head I wanted to hide
Thick in Zuleo I've got no pride
Going out oh the shame
We started to laugh
Cos we all looked the same

Who Made You? God Made Me

The other visitor was the Parish Priest who could pop in any time to ask us questions on the catechism. This little book was a collection of questions and answers put together by the Church about God and the Bible, which we had to learn parrot fashion and God help you if you got your question wrong. Hold out your hand.

Another person who liked to make her presence felt was the Headmistress of St Laurences School where we were based and who really had nothing to do with us but must have felt it was her school so she could rule the roost over everybody. Nobody argued with her because she was a Nun and in Roman Catholic Schools you were always in awe of Priests and Nuns, so if they said "jump"- you jumped.

I remember that sister Cleavis was not a very nice person who made everybody nervous who was near to her. She was particularly nasty when on staircase duty.

The Black Habit

Is sister Cleaveris on the stairs today?
Yes she is, so stay out of her way
In her long black robes on the staircase she stood
Hidden hands held a long thin wood
Never a word was ever said
She watched and watched

For a broken tread
Oh my god I`m out of line
She glared at you
And you knew the sign
Out of the folds of this long black dress
A whooshing sound
What a mess
Out came the hand
Out came the stick
The back of the legs felt a burning flick
She was cool
She was fast
Weals on your legs
All day would last
But never ever did we see the cane
But blinkin heck!! we felt the pain

Bless me Father

Every Sunday and Holy days we had to attend Mass. On Sundays you had to make your own way and if it was a Holy Day in the week we were lined up two by two in school by your teacher and walked to church.

Our Church was St Werburghs. It is the only Church left in the town centre where people can still attend mass and I think the first Roman Catholic Church to be built when the town became more populated with Irish immigrants.

People came in from everywhere as Birkenhead grew with the new docks and Cammell Laird swelled from a tiny boatyard to a huge Shipbuilders yard, one of the biggest in Great Britain and Europe.

So off to Church we had to march, but on Sunday we had to go under our own steam. We had to attend nine o clock Mass known as the `Children's Mass` and if we were too late for nine o clock we would be in trouble come Monday morning. After the teacher had called the school register she would then call out for the Church attendance and no excuses were accepted. Not there! Hold out your hand!!

I remember in later years we had moved to the Woodchurch Estate when it was still being built and the Sunday buses were only every hour. The bus I had to get was at eight o`clock for me to be at nine o clock Mass. I would be at Central Station at twenty past eight. Mum and Dad went mad when I told them I had hung around until nine that the next week I was told I should go to St Joseph`s Church in Upton. This was quite a walk but lots of people were going to Church, so I had lots of company.

When I went to school on the Monday I had to tell the teacher what hymns were sung, which Priest said what Mass at what time and they didn`t believe you until it was checked out. I don`t think that some teachers liked kids very much and they certainly didn`t trust them.

When we were eight we had to make our First Communion which was the first time we received the little wafer that represented the Body of Christ, prior to that we had to confess our sins to the Priest.

Saturday evening we went to Church entered a cubicle where the Priest sat on the other side of a screen. Supposedly he couldn`t see you. "Bless me father for I have sinned". We then went on to confess all our sins which was very difficult as we didn`t always know what they were but the Priest had said "No one is without sin", We had to believe him so we would say things like, we swore or told lies. We were then given a penance. You will say ten Hail Marys and one Our Father. You would thank the Priest for his forgiveness, kneel in a pew outside the confessional and say your penance.

You were then cleansed enough to receive communion on the Sunday. I know other kids made up their sins as well because we told each other when we got older.

Hospital

When I was eight I had to have my tonsils out because of sore throats and I was taken to The Children's Hospital on Woodchurch Road. I was kept in for two weeks and only Mum or Dad was allowed in for one hour each day.

On the day of the operation (no visitors) all the kids having their tonsils out were lined up on their beds in the corridor outside the theatre, wheeled in and after the removal of their tonsils, wheeled out past the kids waiting to go in, and we could see the blood coming from the throat.

The ones waiting to go in were crying as I was and I was told to stop crying and set an example as I was the oldest. I was eight!! I was wheeled in put on the table a mask put over my mouth and nose and told to breathe in the ether which knocked you out. What I wanted was to pull the mask off my face but the nurses held me down until I went off. It was frightening. I cried for Mum to take me home but she wasn't allowed to take me.

The up side was that I was spoilt for the next two weeks as I could only eat jelly and ice-cream until my throat was better. Comics and books came from everywhere but I have to be honest and say it was not a happy experience and forever after I couldn't go to the dentist because the smell was the same smell of the operating theatre.

Our Richie had to go into hospital for something and he ran away. He climbed down the fire escape in Pyjamas. He was running down Borough Road when he met a pal who was on his order bike. These bikes had big metal type baskets on the front which held all the grocery and butchers orders for the posh people who could afford to have their foodstuffs delivered-Not for them waiting in endless queues. So his pal gave him a lift on the front and they then bumped into a Bobby who gave the poor lad with the bike a clip around the ear and he took Richie back. As you can see kids were not mollycoddled.

St Andrews Square
The Flats
Boys And Girls Come Out To Play

We were back from Welshpool and were given the keys for the flats. It was about 1942 and lived there until I was twelve and if I say it was a great place to live as a kid it certainly was because it was a big playground. No swings or slides. But imagination is a fantastic thing and what we kids had in those years was imagination.

Firstly we had a bombed out Church with a graveyard. We had our own race track. Verandahs to play hide and seek, gardens, no grass, no flowers, and no trees but walls to leap over, a counter when we played shop. We had plenty of room to run around playing Cowboys and Injuns with make believe bows and arrows and make believe horses with reins smacking our backsides on a make believe horse's rump.

On the racetrack we had foot races and some kids had a homemade go-cart which the owner sat on while your mate pushed you around the track. We had old bikes with wobbly wheels ready for the scrap heap. So much of the stuff by the standards of today was absolute rubbish but to us wonderful. We had our own Olympic Games. Our Peggy had a bike which she didn't use any more so it was passed to me and Dad painted it. So on it I learned to ride and from then on I was on it morning noon and night.

Dip, Dip, Dip My Blue Ship

Other games we played were 'Yally Yo' and how we played it was that somebody was dipped to be the chaser and the chaser had to close their eyes and count to a hundred while the rest of us ran and hid. This was a more grown up version of Hide and Seek with the little kids who couldn't leave the flats getting caught fast but the older kids would take ages getting found because they would hide in the Church and the bombed out houses until they could get back to the den without being seen.

Another game was British Bulldog in which the chosen person stood facing all the other kids and then one by one you were called out to try and get past the poor soul in the middle and get to the other side without getting caught. If you did get caught, you joined the man in the middle. We were all called men then, "politically correct" wasn't heard of. So as the middle got crowded it got harder to cross and the last man caught was the winner and the first man caught went into the middle and we started all over again. Sometimes there could have been as many as thirty or forty kids playing and it could take ages to finish the game.

The other game that used to frighten us when we played didn't have a name. A gang of us would head to the Flat Iron, a pub that was on the bend of Conway St and Claughton Rd. It had an entrance on both roads with swing doors straight across facing each other.

So the game went like this. We stood outside usually about six of us and we would dip, dip, dip my blue ship and we went out one by one. Please!! Let me go out first, let me be number one, Oh no!! Please let me be number two and so on until we all had a number and so the game began. Number one would push through the swing door in Conway St run across the pub and run through the other swing door in Claughton Rd. Number two and three would get through without a problem, but by number four or five the pub manager woke up to what was going on and grabbed the next one, gave him or her a clout (no sex discrimination in those days). The ones coming behind still had to go in knowing you were going to get the same If you didn't you were in trouble with your mates. Also depending on the manager he might call the local bobby and you would get another clout and maybe taken home for more punishment. "Thank you officer I will take over now" and Dad would give me the 'look'.

Conway Arms / Flat Iron - Conway Street School
My School from 1951-55.

Games came in seasons. The winter games with lots of running about to keep warm. Skipping with a huge rope was winter or summer and there would be lots of kids running in and out, up and down. `Pitch Patch Pepper` would leave you with very red legs when the rope got you at the back. I can also remember how we were able to have the rope across Conway Street and skip on the main road without a car passing throughout the whole game and this was the main road.

Occasionally a horse and cart might have passed. Summer games were Skipping, Top and Whip, Two Balls mostly played by the girls, Allies and Jacks by the boys, Footie and Cricket of course.

When the weather was bad and we stayed in or when we were too young to stay out late I can remember Dad was always willing to play Shop and Post office and he was always the customer. Half of his mind was reading the Echo and the other half was in my shop.

Before it got dark if he had the money he would send me for two ounces of sweets. We did get pocket money. Our Georgie a shilling, Eddie ninepence, Richie sixpence, and me threepence ,but I always had my little treats when I stayed in with Dad and Mum went off for a natter to her Mums or Auntie Kits.

In those days a silver shilling was twelve pence which is now equivalent to five new p. In those days there were 240 pence to the pound. We also had half crowns worth about thirty new p. Also a ten shilling note was worth 120 old pennies, today fifty new p. All replaced by decimal.

Christmas Is Coming The Goose Is Getting Fat.

One of the first signs that Christmas was coming when I was about eight was Dad was bringing pieces of scrap wood home from the docks and storing them in the empty bedroom and when he had a stock he put the room off limits.

When he wasn't at work we could hear him tapping away in there which went on for weeks. Also over at Uncle Fred's Monty the Goose was getting bigger and fatter.

Monty had been bought as a chick to fatten up for Christmas and he was kept on Auntie Kit`s landing, fenced off from next door. As a chick he was very cute and all the kids who lived in St Andrews Square thought it was great to have a zoo on a veranda. Auntie Kit had a little white dog named Snowie as well. Monty was fed any scraps of food and peelings left from the kitchens. He was very well looked after. All the kids loved him. Plus if Auntie Kit had been baking the kids could be sure of a nibble.

So Monty got bigger, plumper and stronger. He also got nasty and to get into the flat you had to climb over the fence and past Monty who, if he didn`t like you would peck at your legs or any part he could peck at. Actually when I think of it, if we all had a goose as a guard on our gates I think any burglar would think twice about climbing over, so I might get one.

So on came Christmas and Monty disappeared from the landing. We knew not where until Christmas day.

Dinner time and there we were all sat around the table, the Wiggins and the Kellys all in our Christmas best waiting for the best meal of the year. Then Uncle Fred comes in from the kitchen with the loveliest bird we had ever seen. Oh no!!! There lay Monty defrocked, deplucked and deheaded, when it sunk in the kids went silent, "Come on tuck in" said Uncle Fred but we couldn`t. We were in floods of tears. Poor Monty!!! And when word got out all the kids in the flats went into mourning.

Nowadays all the poultry comes ready dressed as they say but back then if you wanted poultry you had to do all the work yourself. Uncle Fred thought to give everybody a treat by buying a goose and rearing it for Christmas but hadn`t counted on it becoming a pet. I think the only ones who tucked into poor Monty were the grownups. Our Peggy is a vegetarian (not heard of in those days) she was just someone who wouldn`t eat meat- just the same as my daughter Tracey in later years.

So back to Dad who had been knocking away in the empty room. He would be in there for a couple of weeks and finally on Christmas morn there would be an assortment of toys for us. One year there was a cot and Mum had made some bedding. There was a doll (probably the same doll the lads pulled the head off which put me off dolls forever). Another year he made me a desk and when I played school with the kids I could be teacher. I liked that school better than the one I had to go to. There would be things for the lads- bows and arrows, swords, cricket bats and stumps which were probably put away for the summer.

So with the presents we got from the Grotto we did really well.

Sing, Sing A Song

Another part of Christmas was family visits, neighbours popping in and the sing songs.

Everybody had to have a party piece maybe a little ditty or tell a joke but mostly people sang a song. The singer sang the song once and then we would all join in and sing the song again. We all learned the words of songs very young because as there was no television we listened to the radio which would be on all day long. People sang a lot in those days and even now when a group of my friends get together we love a good singsong.

There was a lot of talent at these parties and my Mums brothers Dickie, Billy, and Peter had wonderful voices. They could sing together or alone. Uncle John could sing as well but he had died young. His song was `Begin the Beguine`. Frankie and Eddie were the same age as us and still kids, I don`t remember if they had a party pieces.

Come on Sue sing `You`ll never know`
Hey George give us `Just a rose in a garden of weeds`.
And Fred ` Barefoot days`
Tinkle the ivories Kit and we`ll all join in
What about Dickie, Billy and Peter, bring on Joseph Locke lads
Who`s next? who`s next? What about the kids?
Eddie `A your adorable`
Irene `B you`re so beautiful`
Eddie `C your a cutiful of charms`
That`s smashing kids.

And so went on the evening, everyone singing their heads off. The pubs the same, singing all night and when they closed you could still hear the singing as they stood outside reluctant to go home.

The singers of the day were the same ones who had sung for people through the war- Vera Lynn, Anne Shelton (Mums favourite) and lots of others who had entertained the troops on the frontline and helped to keep up their spirits away from home.

At this time a new radio station named Radio Luxemburg began broadcasting and we were listening to new singers. With the Americans who came over to help fight the war and were stationed all over England we were introduced to a very different type of music.

A very young Frank Sinatra, Dean Martin and Perry Como and the Big Band sound. We had never heard anything like it. We would be glued to the station when it was on which would be late at night because of the time lapse. There were no satellites in those days to join us up.

So now everybody was singing to a different style and Dean Martin and Perry Como were the favourites of Mum`s brothers. Frank Sinatra who gave the women romance could sing a ballad like no other. Billie entered a talent show that was travelling the country- `The Carroll Levis Discoveries` (just like the X factor today) and it was held at the Ritz cinema. Uncle Billy won and Carroll Levis who was the Simon Cowell of the day wanted to take him away, and make him a star. I think Uncle Billie might have got stage fright and wouldn't go but he had the talent of any of the tenors that were around then. I sometimes wonder if he ever regretted it. .

Mum`' brothers Richard and Peter
both of them Cooks in the army

Richard married Marianne Rieke who was German and they met when Dickie was stationed in Germany just after the war. Peter married Monica Bastow.

William (Billy) fifteen

Billy lied about his age to get into the Army. He married Margaret Byrd.

THE SINGERS

Richard, Peter, Frankie all ready for a song

*Billy (Dobby) as he was known with his Horse and cart.
He is the one in the white shirt.*

We Wish You A Merry Christmas

So Christmas as I remember was of waking up Christmas morning to the toys that Dad had made and our stockings hanging on the headboard with an orange, apple and some nuts with any little thing Mum and Dad could afford.

We would get dressed in our Christmas clothes worn just once for the grotto. We would play for a while waiting for neighbours to pop in and soon we would go visiting family such as Nan to see everybody who was there. Maybe the young lads were still in the army and couldn't get home, that was sad.

So many men had been killed that their families struggled to give the kids a nice Christmas, but I don't really remember the sad times. I think it was the adults who really missed the ones who weren't there.

When all the visiting was over it was time for the Christmas Dinner and we all gathered around the table the Wiggins and the Kellys for the feast of the year. Turkey (no more Monty) was eaten with all the trimmings and afterwards we played games. In the evening more people popping in, someone on the piano and a sing song would finish the day.

Over to Boxing Day you would catch up with anyone you hadn't seen the day before and everything would start again. The grownups and the kids as I remember spent Christmas together and that's how I hope my kids remember their Christmases.

Winter Washday Blues

What you could be pretty sure of was that sometime over the holiday there would be snow and the kids would shout hurrah!! And the Mums would cry oh no!! The kids would be thinking `let the winter fun begin` and the Mums would be thinking `how do we keep everything dry and warm and get the washing dry.` What was a lot of fun to us was a big headache to the grownups.

Women had to boil water on the top of the cooker to do their weekly washing. No such things as washing machines or dryers. Everything was scrubbed by hand and wrung out by brute strength. If you were lucky you had a mangle which was a hand turned machine with rollers in which you had to push your washing through between the rollers, turn the handle and squeeze out the excess water,- pure hard work.

The kids would be playing in the snow having a ball not worrying about wetting their feet and clothes- not our problem. But playtime could be interrupted by your mum shouting for you to come in and turn the handle "Oh no Mum I'm playing" "You get in now or you'll be in for the day". So in you went and for the next hour or so you turned the handle while your
Mum pushed the washing through the rollers, itching to be out with your mates.

But that was when the snow was fresh. Soon the weather would become so cold the snow would freeze solid which was smashing for slides. But getting up to go to school or work was another thing.

Lots of men who worked outside (which was probably more than half of the workforce) were laid off so no money was coming in.

The kids in school were freezing. We would have wet feet, wet socks and chilblains caused through not having the best of footwear. No central heating, maybe not much breakfast if your dad had no work. You were given a bottle of milk in school (not heated) to feed you up but it was freezing cold and you had to drink it.   I hated milk then and I hate it now.

The years during the war and after were very hard but harder still for the parents trying to look after their kids. But we kids didn`t know how hard it was. We just played, went to school played some more and had a very good time and never worried about a thing.

As the years went by things started to get better- more work for the men and now women went to work too. Not the cleaning jobs that married women had had to settle for. Now they started in the factories.

I remember Mum wanted to go out to work at a factory called Norman Foods but Dad didn`t want her to as he thought she should stay at home and look after us. That was the way it happened in those days, man the breadwinner, woman the homemaker. However Mum was determined and kept on until Dad relented and said she could go for as long as it took for her to make enough money to buy a bedroom suite which was what Mum wanted. I think Mum was about thirty four at the time and she worked from that day until she was sixty five and had to retire.

In Norman Foods they canned fruit mostly English fruit. I think they were plums, damsons, blackcurrants, raspberries and apples but it was very hard work and the women continually had their hands in cold water doing to the fruit whatever they had to do before it got to the tins. The hours were long as we're all working hours in those days. Mum left the house at a quarter past seven in the morning and walked to work for half past. No car to take her, she would walk home at five thirty hail, rain and snow.

As I got older I used to walk to meet her and it was lovely to see her come into view but in the dark nights she would tell me off for coming and for a few days I wouldn`t go. But then I would take a chance and set out. I remember feeling very grown up meeting Mum from work.

Dad worked on the docks loading and unloading ships that came in from all over the world. To get work he would have to line up in the pen very early in the morning at half past six and there would be hundreds of men all hoping for a ship that needed working. It was very iffy, because if only a couple of ships wanted loading and there was more men than was needed you had to hope the foreman liked you enough to pick you and if he didn`t tough!!!. You had no work that morning and all those men without had to do the same thing and line up again at one o clock and the next day. In the meantime a ship would go out and the men from that ship would join you in the pen.

So there would be a huge queue of Dockers looking for work. But if there were a few ships in, that needed to be loaded quickly because of other ships sitting out in the Mersey, waiting to come in, Dockers had to work day and night unloading the cargo coming from abroad. They then had to load the cargo to get the ships back out, and this would mean good pay packets, but there wouldn't be much time at home.

The only time there was full employment was during the war when there was a manpower shortage when all the men were off fighting. Dockers were exempt from the army if they had families and were past a certain age because they were needed at home to keep the docks moving.

Working the docks and factories were very dangerous jobs. They were the first places to be bombed by German planes and people were killed in their thousands but as I have said I do not remember any of this.

First The Tide Rushes In,
Cockles And Mussels Alive, Alive Oh!

Days out we had lots. In the summer months if the weather was dry we were taken to Moreton Shore. I can remember going to Moreton from the age of five or six and still going until I was fifteen or more. Now that might not sound very exciting to the kids of today but I can tell you it was.

People came from all over the Wirral and Liverpool. This was in the heyday of the Ferry boats and every quarter of an hour one arrived at Woodside where all the Scousers packed the buses and headed for Moreton Common. The buses would be full by the time it got to our bus stop, so we had to get up early to get on one and when we did, all the kids went upstairs while the grownups stayed down. Going to Moreton on the bus was all part of the day out because we sang all the way,- all the war songs, they were all we knew, 'Pack up your troubles in your old kitbag' 'It's a long way to Tipperary' 'Hang up your washing on the Siegfried line' 'Run rabbit run rabbit run, run, run' to name a few.

When Moreton finally came into view we would all cheer and lift the roof off the bus with the noise then scramble off and run down the road up and over the embankment- all the Mums shouting "Get back here and help with these bags". But we were gone. The race was on to be the first one to shout "The tides in" or out whatever the case maybe. It was a big thing especially for the lads if they won.

We then made our way onto the Common but we then had a problem. Where had Dad and Uncle Fred pitched the tent!!! They always went earlier than us on their bikes to be sure of a pitch and tried to get to the same spot but there would be hundreds of tents and most of them were white or brown. Ours was brown, so if they weren't where we thought they should be we were in a mess. Imagine looking for a car in a car park and someone else had parked it and all the cars were pretty much the same size and colour. So while we would be looking for the tent, scouts would be sent out to look for us. Then they would get lost. We would find the tent, get told off and be sent to look for the scouts. I suppose it was a bit like Laurel and Hardy but while we were all looking for each other we met up with pals who also went there every week.

Lots of tents on Moreton shore
Is there room for just one more?
We`ll squeeze you in never fear
Here`s a spot over here"
Out came the butties for us to eat
Meat paste or cheese what a treat
Is anyone going for hot water?
To make the tea I suppose I oughta
Over the grass past the loo,
Oh my god! Look at the queue
What the heck it doesn't matter
There`s always a mate to have a natter
Are you digging for cockles today?
Deffo when the water`s away
We`ll be setting up cricket on the sand,
If you want give us a hand
So after cricket here comes dad
We`re going cockling grab a bag
Grab your spade we`ve locked the tent, (Huh!!)
Hurry up it`s time we went
Out on the sand the water ahead
Looking for spouts that`s a cockle bed
Down we dig to bring them up
We fill the bags to the top,
The tide has turned, time to go back
All the grownups carry a sack
Look at that lot says Kitty and Sue!!!!!
You`d think we had nothing better to do
We`ll be washing, cleaning, pickling, the lot
We`ll deserve a bottle of the you know what,
Isn`t it great the water`s in
Cossies on, all in for a swim
　　　　But me

Bloomin eck the water`s cold
You're just a sissie you`ve got to be bold,
I`m getting out, I`ll stand on the edge
Watch that drop me mother said
If you fall down there you will drown
How can I Mum with you around
Don`t be cheeky you`ll get a clout
Get back in,   Or
I`ll keep you out   huh!!!

Mike   *Eddie*
Frannie   *Me*   *Richie*

The two babies Billie and Catherine Wallace are
Auntie Mags twins.

Peggie, Me holding Robert, and Uncle Fred

Frannie with Meryl Hulse Dickies sister

When the school holidays came and Dad and Uncle Fred were at work, Mum and Auntie Kit would take us for days out and we would take a picnic and go to the beach for the day.

As I have said money dictated where we went but I remember one time when we went to West Kirby. I only remember the younger kids being there so the older ones must have been working. Peggy, Freddie and our Georgie had probably left school at fourteen. I didn't have a bathing suit so I wouldn't go in, so Auntie Kit had a bright idea.

Best pals
Mum and Aunt Kit

The Tablecloth And The Cossie

"Shall we take the kids to the beach, Kit?
And get them out the house.
Have you got the butties done
Pity we can`t take that scouse".
"Is everything packed in the bags, Sue"?
"No there`s only the tablecloth".
"You and that blinkin cloth Sue
Now have we got the lot"?

"I bet you`ve got your needle and thread
Your just as bad as me
I don`t suppose you`ll use them"
"Just you wait and see".
Down to the Shore,
The weather is hot
The kids all go in for a swim
All except one, the littlest one,
Who's got nowt to wear to go in.
"Go in your Knickers" says Auntie Kit
you're going to miss all the fun"
"No I won`t says the littlest one
I want a cossie to put on"
"What can we do" says Auntie Kit
Who sees the little one cry
There must be some way around it
Something I can try
Out comes the needle
Out comes the thread
And up comes the cloth
that`s keeping the sand out of the bread
Now Auntie Kit is good at the sewing
She`s making a wreck of Sues cloth
Don`t worry says Kit
I`ll soon make it fit
To wear as a cossie instead
So lo and behold what do you think
In twenty minutes or so
A little two piece
To give to her niece
Coloured, bright yellow and pink.

We didn't get to West Kirby very often and the only time I went to Hilbre Island was on Freddie Wiggin's shoulders. I was about seven. I remember walking into slimy mud and crying because it seemed very deep and my big cousin picking me up, mud and all and putting me on his back. Later when he bought himself a motor bike he would take me for rides on the back.

On a good pay week and if we were off school we would be taken to New Brighton Pleasure beach which was a smaller funfair than Blackpool but had a Tower that was taller than Blackpools, and a beautiful pier with penny arcades and cafes and little fun rides for the little kids. New Brighton heaved with people and there were shops everywhere the very opposite to what it is now. Gone now are the beautiful pier and the big outdoor fairground also the lovely outdoor swimming pool where they held the beauty competitions every year. The pool was huge and had high diving boards which the lads would jump off to impress the girls.

The Tower was dismantled before I was born, but left on the bottom, the Ballroom was still intact. It had a huge dance floor. The

place would throb with live.music. This was where most people seemed to meet and start dating and eventually marry their chosen partner. This was a step up from the Penny Hop I mentioned earlier. But on our day out we were heading for the BIG fair. The fairground was in gardens which surrounded the tower. The Tower above the ballroom had gone when I went to New Brighton possibly for the War effort.

New Brighton Tower with the Ballroom below

70

Dad's Ship's In

"I`ve got an extra few bob Sue
shall we take the kid`s to the fair?"
"Yes` let`s have a treat George,
The train will get us there"
"Shall I make some butties, what do you think?"
"No, we`ll have a bag of chips
And get some pop to drink".
Off the train down to the fair
Lots of rides, they`re everywhere
Dodgem cars, merry go round
The paddle boats   Hope we don`t drown!!
Helter Skelter. The big yellow Boots
that go higher and higher and loop the loop
The lads like the Dodgems don`t they go fast
What`s that bang?!!!someone`s crashed
But I like the Merry go round
Up and down and off the ground.
Everyone onto the figure of eight
Terrified! We go through the gate
The train it sits on very small rails
"Let me off" everyone wails
But up and up and over the top
Keep tight hold you might fall off,
Faster and faster down we go
We`ll hit the ground down below
Up and over again and again
Until we have to get off the train
Our legs like jelly we tremble and shake
Down the steps we`ll never make
Never again we all cry
Dads says" back on for another ride".
                    Yes please!

71

We're All Going On A Summer Holiday

It`s now about 1948. There is more work, more money so Mum and Dad decided to take us on holiday to Rhyl. You might think Rhyl!! but we were only used to days out to Bidston Hill, Birkenhead Park, Arrowe Park, Moreton shore. Meols and West Kirby too, if Dad had a good week in work and could afford the bus fare. Mum was still working for a bedroom suite and wasn`t parting.

Right Kids, we are going on holiday! On holiday!!! Where are we going Dad? "Rhyl" said Dad or just outside to Palins camp. We are taking the tent and we will sleep in it for a week." Mum said "We must be crackers, what if it rains? We`ll be as a snug as a bug in a rug so stop worrying, Dad replied.

Dad and Georgie went out to Rhyl the day before us to set up camp. They were going on bikes and tied to their crossbars was all the equipment we would need for the week- six foot long tent poles, a rolled up tent tied onto the poles, a kettle and a pan were dangling from the poles too. Tied onto the back of the bikes Dad and Georgie each had a bag with all sorts of paraphernalia inside.

What a send off the neighbours gave them as they wobbled off to cycle the fifty odd miles to Palins camp. Mum`s final words were "You`ll never get there" "Yes we will, and you make sure you get on that train tomorrow". Georgie was probably about fourteen so this was a huge bike ride as he hadn`t travelled out of the Wirral never mind Wales but he wouldn`t have missed it for anything.

Wooodside train Station behind the bus, where we got the train to Rhyl also one of the Corporation buses that took us to Moreton nearly every week.

That night we had to sleep at Auntie Kits and Uncle Freds, I think it was because we had no Kettle, pans or cutlery. It was all in Rhyl surmising they had gotten there. Nobody had telephones so they couldn`t call to say they had safely arrived. (Auntie Cissie, Dads sister had a phone but she lived in Bebington and Auntie Kit didn`t get on with her oldest sister but that`s another story).

So next morning we set off on the train, Mum, Eddie, Richie and me. We got on the Train at Woodside Station, now demolished for Municipal Buildings and a `You know what!!   Holidays, steam trains, this was going to be special. As we got on the guard blew his whistle, the train let out a huge Woo, Woo with steam puffing out everywhere, doors slammed and away we went waving to anyone who waved to us.

We passed through Rock Ferry where we used to go to see Auntie May Uncle Jo, Joey, Rene and Alan our cousins on the electric train once a month. Mum said "Give them a wave" as we passed close to Railway Road where they lived. They didn`t know we were waving so we told them on one of the many postcards we had to send while we were on HOLIDAY!!! We passed through Chester then along the Welsh Coast "Look Mum there`s the sea, here`s Talacre, and here comes Rhyl ". At the station we make sure we don`t leave anything, "Oh look there`s your Dad." Dad piles the luggage onto his trusty steed (his bike) and our Georgie sits me on his crossbar. "How far is it to the tent?" Well you`ve got a little bit of a walk through the town but you won`t notice it, replies Dad and we didn`t because along the prom was all the exciting things Rhyl had to offer.

Firstly we had to get the luggage to the tent which was set up in Palins camp. This was a field full of tents and a few caravans in which people who had a couple of bob were staying.

At one end of the field close to us was a chemical toilet which sat in a sentry box. Behind the box on the other side of a hedge was a field full of cows. Now we had seen cows before but usually we were on the bus going to Arrowe Park and quite a bit away but these were just a length of an arm away and huge, "Oh my God George what if they get out they`ll trample us" says Mum, "Don`t be daft they are only cows they won`t harm you" Dad replied, "Well I hope not. If they do we are off home" said a haughty Mum "Don`t worry Mum" said Roy Rogers, Hoppalong Cassidy and Billy the Kid we`ll round them up" "Okay we`ll stay then".

So we went into the tent to see the sleeping arrangements. Dad was to sleep by the entrance with Mum at the other end. They were there to keep out intruders and the cold night air. We four safely in the middle all cuddled up to each other ,not that we had much choice.

The next morning we were up and rearing to go but first we had to wash and get ready. So off to the tap for water which was freezing cold and I mean cold I think we hoped to get away with a cats lick but not with Mum looking on "Make sure you get a proper wash or you`ll be back on that train" I think she would have been glad to go because this holiday was pretty primitive but not to us.

All we had to do was wash in the freezing cold water and then enjoy ourselves but Mum and Dad had to keep the bedding dry and cook on a tiny primus stove. Poor Mum must have had aches and pains everywhere sleeping on the very hard ground, but she put up with it to give us a lovely time, which it was until a few days into the holiday.

On our first day we walked into Rhyl after having a hearty breakfast to keep us going for the day. Rhyl wasn't that much different to New Brighton but bigger so it took us longer to walk around and make our mind up as to what we would spend our daily allowance on.

Before we came away we had been given money by Aunts and Uncles to spend so we went into the Penny Arcade on the slot machines. I remember being very lucky and having a pocketful of coppers and it reminded me of VE day when I was carried to the Town Hall on Dad's back and everyone was putting coppers in my hand because of my little Union Jack dress. So now I had coppers to put into the slots in which I probably fed the lot but not to worry. There was still a lot going on- Fairground rides, paddling in the sea, games on the sand, but the best bit was when a bike, a three wheeler was hired for me to ride up and down the prom. Such Freedom.

At the end of the day we then had to walk back to the tent but we loved it especially when we came to a little chippie cafe and we were taken in and sat on high stools and Dad said "Chips and fish for everyone" we looked at each other, Is it Grotto day? Is Father Christmas behind us? "No" said Dad "We are on holiday".

So for the next few days we loved it, but then came a change in the weather. Overnight storms came in and we woke very early to loud bangs and the tent being blown down and when we went outside the wooden toilet block was heading our way. The cows had broken out of the fields and were running about in panic. "Quick" says Dad, "Pull the tent out of the way before the toilet hits it". When the lads saw the cows they answered the bugle call and started to round up the cattle which was to be a fantastic end to the holiday for them. Fearless they were!! They remembered everything they had seen at the MICKEYPOPS.

The people who were in the caravan close to us took us in and gave us something to eat. Everything we had was wrapped up because it was all soaking wet. There was no way we could stay. So poor Dad and Georgie had a long ride home with a heavier load then when they had ridden out because of the soaking tent. But we were alright on the train. It was a sad ending to the holiday but certainly one to remember.

Palin's camp still survives but it isn't the camp we knew. It's a huge holiday park now. But our Cafe has gone.

This could almost be me on a three wheeler

Uncles and Aunts

Dad was very close to his brothers and sisters and liked us to visit them or they visited us.

Uncle Ted

My favourite Uncle was Uncle Ted
One tooth in his mouth
Just a little hair on his head
Always laughing always fun
His toothless smile like a breaking sun
But Uncle Ted he liked a drop
And when at work on the dock
Into a corner he would creep
Would often be found fast asleep
And many a time on a ship would snooze
Then disappear on a` luxury cruise` (not very)
"Maggie`s and Sarah`s here George, looking for Ted
Never been home, never slept in his bed."
"He probably had a drop too much
It won`t be long until he phones up
Auntie Mag had had them before
Phone calls from British ports of call
She also had had one from France
He really led her a merry dance
But with Uncle Ted she couldn`t be mad
He hadn`t grownup, still a lad

But the magic of this lovely man
A tin of paints and a pad
So he could draw
Whatever he saw
And into water colours they became
No two pictures ever the same
Memories for all to share
That made you wish you had been there

As years went by Sarah married
Off to Australia she was carried
And for years asked her Dad and Mum
To Australia would they come?
Finally when they reached retirement age
In Tasmania a home was made
With their daughter happy at last
His travelling days were past   ALMOST
Auntie Maggie was laid to rest
They picked a spot they thought the best
Outside Devonport in Birkenhead
The river Mersey ran past her head
Put us here when we are gone
Lying together in the sun

A letter came for Dad to say
Uncle Ted had passed away
As Dad read the letter tears in his eyes
He was in for a great surprise
Sarah had written "Don`t be sad
A happy ending for my Dad
We had booked him onto a flight
He should have arrived with us that night
Surprise surprise! He wasn`t there
It seems that he was still in the air
Even dead he could still get lost
Travelling Australia at no extra cost
But Mum she waited patiently
I know he`ll soon be here with me

*Uncle Ted, Sarah and
Auntie Maggie*

Years later I went to Australia and visited Sarah who had moved to Brisbane. She told me the story again and I then went on to Tasmania to see the grave of my lovely Uncle and Aunt. They are buried in a place called Birkenhead lying close to the River Mersey and I thought how great that this man who had worked on the docks on the Mersey all his working life should follow his daughter to Australia and spend eternity in a place called Birkenhead and lay beside the Mersey.

I also wondered who the person was who named this place Birkenhead.

After Auntie Maggie died Sarah, Dennis and Uncle Ted travelled to Brisbane where he died and it was then on his journey back to Tasmania his coffin was put on the wrong plane for his final trip.

Uncle Albert

Uncle Albert was Dad`s youngest brother and he was another character .He had to go into the Army and gave everyone a bad time but I still loved him because he was always acting the fool with us kids.

Uncle Albert and the Army

Uncle Albert went into the army
He hated every bit
The spit and polish got him down
The marching in full kit
Up at dawn no mod cons
Washing in cold water
Dear Mam I have to say
This army is pure murder,
I hate the bloody army Mam
But it does no good to moan"
Nobody likes the army Son,
Does the army know your home?
They take him to the station
They put him on the train
And every blinking time they do,
He jumps back off again
Into the glasshouse Kelly
Your punishment you will take
You're just a bloody coward lad,
No sir it`s jankers I can`t take
So Albert went to prison,
You`ll get what you deserve
What will the army do with him
He`s got no blooming nerve
He stood before the captain,
The captain said to him
You`ll go in bomb disposal lad,
the future`s looking grim
Thank you sir, no more bull,
No standing on parade
Would it be ok sir if I made a start today?

So into bomb disposal,
Each day it comes so fast
But is our Albert bothered
Today might be his last.
It`s not that he`s a coward,
He never could fit in.
But now he`s in disposal
It`s made a man of him
And now he`s the captain right hand man
Or so he says to us
We take it with a pinch of salt,
It doesn`t do to fuss

Didn't We Have A Lovely Day The Day Went To...?

So the war is well over. Life is getting better and I am getting older. I am about ten and being allowed to go further afield with my friends Josie Owens, Anne Birch and Norma Nugent and our first port of call was Birkenhead Park. Now Birkenhead Park was right on our doorstep but we only knew the bits that we were taken to, the swings and play area but now we could explore it all and we did.

Up until now our playground had been the flats and the Church cemetery but this park was serious stuff. It was huge. It wasn`t one park it was two and as we got to know our way around we found that by going through the bottom park into the top park and out the other end we could find our way onto Bidston hill, down past the windmill into the pine woods, out onto any of the roads that surrounded the hill. This would be the same as the kids today in Rock ferry finding their way to Eastham bluebell woods.

At this time by Bidston Hill the houses about were few and far between.

Now being allowed more freedom the game of `Yally Yo` took on a new dimension. We would travel miles to keep from getting caught. The catcher would get fed up after a while and call a truce and for a while we would play together until the catcher decided to start up again and grab us while our guard was down. In those days if it was dry we were never in. We were thrown out with the cry "get from under my feet ". So out we were thrown until our tea was ready but if it was wet we went into each others houses to play games.

Now we could go on buses and trains, another world opened up. I remember being given Tuppence to go around the Oxton circle on the bus discovering new places, probably very tame by today`s standard but we did get to know our way about on these adventures. The kid`s today are very restricted by our standards as year by year we were allowed more freedom.

We would walk over the four Bridges now reduced to two and walk along to Seacombe then along the prom to New Brighton. If we had any money we had a little go on the fair, but if we didn`t we would carry on walking to Harrison Drive paddling in the water as we went. The sand and water were really clean and not yet polluted.

Tea In A Jam Jar

I was also now allowed to walk along on my own to my Nan`s who lived in Vernon Place a short walk from St Andrews Square. I loved going and went a lot but Mum would tell me, "Don`t eat your Nan`s rations as she has big lads to feed" but when I got there she would always offer me something. I would say no to anything that was on the ration but she would always make me have a cup of tea. Nan still had the lads at home and so dishes were always getting broke. Nan was always buying cups but sometimes she wouldn`t have enough and she would say I have only got a jam jar. I didn`t care because the very hot stewed tea with Connie onnie milk in a jam jar sweetened with a bit of sugar I loved. I would try it at home but it never tasted as good as my Nans.

So all in all we had a fantastic time living in the Square. Change was to come.

The Woodcurch

After the war a huge building project was started all over the country to replace all the houses and businesses blown up in the war and it also meant the council could knock down the very old housing that had very poor living conditions.

As houses were built and finished, people moved into them. We were offered a house on the Mount estate and I remember Mum, Auntie Kit, our Peggy and me going to see it. I think it was in Cheviot Road but for some reason Mum didn't take it and she was eventually offered the Woodchurch estate. Again we four went to look at it and Mum accepted it and within weeks Auntie Kit was offered one and she said yes. I don't think Dad and Uncle Fred were bothered where they lived as long as the women were happy but once they saw the houses they were thrilled. We lived in 53 Orrets Meadow Rd and Auntie Kit 149 Hoole Rd and right away I loved ours.

Although I missed the flats and friends very much (Anne Birch moved up later) all the kids were in the same boat and we were all looking for friends so it was very easy to settle down.

You Always Find Me Out In The Country

The first memory I have is of fields, beautiful green fields. Orrets Meadow was then the last road before the greenery and I remember the fields were covered in huge dog daisies in the summer. Even the buttercups were big because these fields had been pasture land so had been well fed by the cattle that had grazed on them. Then the second memory is the lovely house, our own garden and actually going upstairs to bed.

Me On the Woodchurch in Uncle Fred's Garden

The only houses I had been in where they went upstairs to bed were Auntie May's, Auntie Maggie's and Auntie Cissie's who I thought were rich because they went upstairs. Uncle Jack and Auntie Cissie also had French windows in their house leading onto the garden so we kids assumed they were loaded. Auntie Kit didn't 'get on' with her big sister as sisters don't. She thought she was a bit of a snob so it was a bit of an occasion if we all went to see her in Bebington.

Auntie Cissie

Aunt Cissie was Dad`s well off sister
As she liked to make it known
Uncle Jack was a coachbuilder
And the house they had was their own
A black telephone stood proud in the hallway
She polished and rubbed till it shone
Mum and Aunt Kit walked on past it
They never would ever let on
She said her profession was nursing
Aunt Kit said ". Auxiliary
She gives herself airs and graces
Who`s she think she kidding, not me"
She never was generous with money
In fact she really was quite mean
And if a child should visit
No pocket money ever was seen
Her house had lovely French windows
They were nice should you want to walk through
"Would you like to stroll around the garden?
But the pair would reply "No thank you"
The other thing Aunt Cissie did
Was grow her own tomatoes
She stood them on the tabletop
Just like a bunch of roses
"Help yourself" Said Auntie Ciss
We pick them by the ton"

Mum and Auntie Kit sat there
And ate every single one
Auntie Cissie stood there watching
Her lips were quite drawn in

And when the bowl was empty
No more did she put in
Dad was out in the garden
Uncle Jack said the vegetables had blight
So far he`d had no carrots and onions
And not a tomato was in sight
So that was our Auntie Cissie
She was such a terrible snob
She forgot where it was that she came from
because Uncle Jack had a couple of bob.

I don`t think Auntie Cissie was very mean just careful. I do remember her giving me coppers for sweets. She was probably saving her money for when they emigrated.

The McAllister's emigrated to New Zealand when I was about ten so out of the three cousins Jackie, Teddie and Rita we must have quite a few relatives out there.

Back to the Woodchurch to our lovely house and garden. Dad was in heaven out in the countryside which he loved. Now he had his own garden which very soon was getting dug up and turned over but what he discovered was lots of clay not suitable for growing. When building the houses all the topsoil had been taken away to dig the foundations so Dad had to find a way to replace the soil as cheaply as possible, in fact for nothing.

So off he went to have a word with the workmen to ask the best way to get his hands on soil and they pointed out little hills that were going to be flattened to build more roads and houses.

When night came in Dad grabbed his spade and wheelbarrow asked me did I want to go with him as there were not many places I didn`t go with him. off we went to a little hill were Dad started digging and filling the wheelbarrow with the lovely black soil. I don`t know how many times we filled the barrow but we went back and forth and then we stopped until the next night.

The next night word had gotten around and there were more wheelbarrows and spades and after a couple of more nights more budding gardeners joined the freebie. But one night a torch was shone on the carryings on and the local Bobby's voice boomed out "ere ere what's going on, be on your way I don't want to see you here again" and there was a mad scuffle as everybody tried to get out of the way. Back home Mum went mad "You'll get yourself locked up and you are not taking her with you again. Dad had to come up with another idea to help his garden soil. So he decided to lay low for a couple nights and leave the soil and go and collect cow flop to dig into the clay instead. Cow flop is wonderful stuff for the garden.

There were lots of cows around and the farmers used to put straw in the gate ways so as the cows left the fields and did their droppings on the straw it was collected to put back into the fields as manure. As night fell again Dad assured Mum he was not going to dig for soil. I don't know if she believed him but I did "Are you coming pet to give me a hand" so off we went. Now you have to remember that I knew nothing about cows, fields and country life and I trusted my Dad totally so when he told me we were only picking up straw and soil I believed him and when he said dig in I did, Mum's shovel in one hand and pushing the dung on the shovel with the other, Dad saying 'good girl we'll have lovely veggies and flowers in the summer'

When we got home and Mum got a whiff of us I found out what I had been shovelling. That was the end of my nightly trips for cow flop. But not the end of hill digging and back we went after a couple of nights but as we got nearer there was one man digging. Dad recognised him as the bobby who had chased us all. As Dad got close he said "Good evening officer" and started to dig. The bobby said nothing. What could he say!!!!

So as time went on we had a beautiful garden. A little lawn was surrounded by different flowers, the ones that became my favourite's bright orange Marigolds and Gypsy grass. At the back was the vegetable patch and on the side a little patch for me where I grew strawberries. I don`t remember being very good, I think I only got one or two. Around the little front garden Dad put a tiny privet hedge which he never let grow above about twelve inches and by the front door steps there was a little drop down onto the garden so he put in three steps built of stone. They were lovely.

Years and years later I went to look at the house and I was very happy to see the steps were still there.

Going to school from the Woodchurch Estate was good fun because there weren`t any schools on the Estate and so we had go to our own schools by special buses. This was a good way to meet and make friends and that was how I met Lily Cruise. She went to the same school but was in an upper class because she was a bit older.

Lily was the girl who went to Ireland for the whole summer holidays and passed me her pen-pal who was a boyfriend in Ireland and I think she was fed up with him. I have to admit I used to write little porkies to impress my pen pal such as my Father was in shipping, which he was being a dock worker but the impression I was giving was he owned the docks. I also told him I went to a private school. In the end I had to stop writing because there was talk about him visiting Lily`s parents and neither Lily or me wanted him to, me because of my sins catching up with me and Lily because she had her eye on someone else.

One of our Richie`s mates, Ray, fancied her and she likewise fancied him. One of the ways he tried to impress her was to nearly frighten her to death.

At that time there were no shops, schools, or churches on the estate but we had a priest, Father Cocoran, and it was his job to start a fund for the building of a new Church (which later became St Michaels and all Angels). Lily`s Mum was a devout Catholic and volunteered Lily to help so I went with her. Father Cocoran`s Church was in Landican Cemetery which was very eerie in the middle of winter, particurlarly at seven o clock at night walking down past the graves.

But we had to help the priest put out the prayer books for a service. As we huddled together to keep out the cold we tried to ignore the dark. We certainly didn't want to look at the gravestones because still fresh in my memory was the story Dad had told our lads about the two Dockers who had had a bet that one of them wouldn't stay in the cemetery all night on his own, so to prove one of them would they both went to the gates. The brave one climbed over and what he had to do was drive a tent pole into the ground by a grave which he did but he didn't pull his overcoat out of the way and as he hammered the tent pole in he also hammered in his coat. As he tried to stand up his coat was trapped and in his imagination he probably thought he was being held by the dead! God love him, and when they opened the gates the next morning he was found dead and his hair was white as snow.

Now you might find many things wrong with this story but when we walked through that grave yard we believed every word of it and I cursed our Richie who repeated it to me. Now back to Lily and Ray having a fancy for each other. So there we were bravely walking down the path with a little light shining from the church and the Father standing there all in black making us more scared. Suddenly floating between the graves were two white apparitions making a wooing noise in and out of the stones ` woo woo` and then "Hello hello, we are coming to get you" "Oh no you are not" and we took to our heels and ran like we had never run before, being chased by these two ghosts until one of them fell over and the other stopped to pick him up just as the priest got to them and unveiled them. So as I said this was Ray`s way of trying to impress Lily and that was one romance that didn't go anywhere.

The lads both got a clip around the ear from Father Cocoran and I probably went home and told Dad what our Richie had done. Revenge is always sweet.

Within a couple of weeks of our moving to the estate Auntie Kit and Uncle Fred moved up too and lived a two minute walk away and it was lovely to be all together again.

While Mum was at work she had bought her bedroom suite and now wanted a nice three piece for her lovely new house. I now had Auntie Kit to go to when I wanted and I bobbed up and down all the time between our house and theirs. Our Peggy was seriously courting Dickie, Freddie had bought a new motorbike and quite often took me on the back. Mike was working and was always buying records by American singers which we now heard more of with Radio Luxemburg playing all the American music at eleven o clock on Sunday night `Top Twenty` was everyone's favourite and then there was Francis who's only aim in life was to torment me and put me off anything I was eating such as Spaghetti in a tin which was just on the market. The first time I was about to eat it he told me it was worms so that was the end of spaghetti for me and he had already put me off cockles which according to him fed on dead men. Lastly there was Susan who was only about two or three and ten years younger than me.

At this time Auntie Kit decided to get a part time job at New Brighton working in the White Cafe so if she worked in the week during the summer holidays I was the one who was chosen to look after Susan which was great because I was paid to. But the best thing was on payday, Frannie, our Richie and me would take Susan on the bus to meet Auntie Kit and she would treat us to chips and a couple of rides on the fair.

Life on the Woodchurch for me was great, I had lots of friends. There was Ann Birch from the flats, Lily, and Glenys Jones. The first friend I made was Sheila Sloan who lived opposite us and together we spent hours roaming the fields and finding new places to explore.

The next two years passed very quickly. I was growing up and had lots more freedom and wandered everywhere. At one time Glenys had a fancy for the paper lad who came from Greasby to deliver the papers, so we had to walk quite often to Greasby so she could drool over him. Then we walked over the fields to watch the lads from the Grammar schools play rugby which was exciting looking at them in their shorts and scrambling about in the mud until one time the visiting team was St Anselms.

Our Eddie was playing and he told us to go home and stop ogling the lads. Maybe he didn`t fancy being ogled by a bunch of thirteen year olds after all he was seventeen and so grown up or thought he was.

The other place we had to go to was Upton Library because Lily fancied the librarian. He was very handsome so I probably liked him too. A shortcut to the Library took us through Upton Cemetery where we had to climb over iron railings into this very old burial ground which was spookier than Landican because it was set right in the middle of nowhere or so it seemed to us. The Woodchurch hadn`t reached this far as yet and the Cemetery was set on the outskirts of Upton village. All the Tombstones were tall and old but nothing must stand in the way of a good ogle!! When we handed in our books we were totally dumbstruck looking at this gorgeous creature but a quick stamp on the new book and that was it for two long weeks.

A thought also has struck me that I spent a lot of time in Cemetaries. The first was St Andrews then into Landican, and then Upton. Much later when I was digging out my family tree I went into St Werburghs graveyard and later Flaybrick where there are lots of Kellys buried. I must confess to loving a good mooch around a graveyard. I have visited a graveyard in Tasmania, Australia and I have dragged my lovely very patient daughter Tracey around Irish burial grounds and churches forever looking for the dead. What does all this say about me?

Still on the Woodchurch and over the road from us lived a lad named Lennie. He brought his mate Brian home from school home with him so Sheila and I took a fancy to them. She fancied Lennie and I fancied Brian. We did a little hand holding and a little kissing around the back of Lennies house where it was just fields. The reason I liked Brian was because he had a bike. So with my old banger and Brian's racer we would go off on rides all over the place, again to places I never knew existed even as far as the Bluebell Woods at Eastham, a lovely place to hold hands and not get caught by your Mum and Dad.

Now I was fourteen and happy. Dad was happy, with his lovely house. Richie had lots of mates and had discovered golf. He played it and made pocket money by caddying for the golfers who had a few bob and paid kids to carry their golf bags for them around the course. Eddie was at college studying hard and our Georgie was in the army. In those days lads were still doing two years National Service and were called up when they were eighteen for two years unless it interfered with college or apprenticeships then they were deferred until they had finished. Then they had to do their service.

Now our Georgie hadn't been a happy bunny when he went into the army because of the fact that he was a terrible snorer and the lads in the barracks gave him a bad time and one time he came home in need of some very fast help.

Our Georgie

"Hi son it's good to see you
When are you going back?"
"Blimey let's get in Mum
It's just a weekend pass"
"Ah son I didn't mean it
Is there something wrong with your face?"
"It's all the lads in the barracks Mum"
"Well it looks a proper disgrace"
"You can tell me all about it
While I make a cup of tea
Your Dad will be glad to see you

He should be in shortly"
"It`s when I go to sleep Mum
That`s when they all attack
They say my snoring is awful"
"It`s cos your on your back"
"They throw all sorts at me
Boots and kit the lot
That`s when I get the bruises
The boots all hit the spot".
Now Mum she got to thinking
How best to help her son
She sat up way past midnight
Nearer half past one
The answer she came up with
Was something he could feel
to stop him falling backwards,
"I know some cotton reels".
So onto string she threaded
The reels for him to wear
Around our George she tied them
To see how he would fare.
So later on we retired
Our Georgie hit the sack
Each time that he turned over
The reels they pushed him back
"Ah thanks they`re great mum
The reels they did the trick
Every time that I went over
They woke me up real quick".
So back to camp went Georgie
Each night it was sheer bliss
Not once did he start snoring
Not one good night was missed
The next two weeks were lovely

The bruises they did heal
Until some clever squaddie
Pinched his cotton reels
Our poor George was so unhappy
His life became a pain
At night he started snoring
They threw the boots again
Is this never ending
Is there no hope for me in sight
Will someone help our Georgie
Help him in his plight
But hope is on the horizon
Georgie`s going home on leave
He`s feeling kinda chirpy
His Mum she will be pleased
"Ah son it`s good to see you
When are you going back"
"Oh not again Mum
It`s just a weekend pass"
"What have you got to tell me
You seemed happy in your note"
"I feel so blinkin good Mum
I really shouldn`t gloat
We've got this new recruit Mum
He saves me all the time
My heart it does go out to him
Cos his snoring is worse than mine

While our Georgie had been doing his National Service he became a film star. Hollywood Star Alan Ladd came to England to make a big block buster war film. To make the film British troops were needed for the marching scenes. Our Georgie`s battalion was chosen and if you look very closely you might just see our `Star` but you would need our Georgie to point Georgie out. But `Alas` he is not with us any longer so you will just have to believe me. He told us about the time he helped `Alan` when he stumbled getting out of a plane, "Are you alright Al?" he asked and then helped him to the Medics. When our Georgie told us this story about his new pal he was very indignant when we started to laugh. But could we really believe that`Shane Shane ` alias Alan Ladd and the biggest Star in Hollywood was our Georgie`s bestest mate. Alan Ladd went back to Hollywood so we couldn`t check with him.

Do you think they are both on that big film set in the sky having the last laugh on us???

Now the three years we spent on the estate was coming to an end. What I hadn`t realised was that Mum wasn`t happy and decided we were going back down town and I have to say I was devastated and Dad was very upset. I didn`t want to leave the estate and all the friends I had made plus the lovely house and garden and green fields. I don`t think the lads were bothered, Georgie in the army hadn`t really lived there, Eddie was a teenager and enjoyed being down town on nights out, Richie had started an apprenticeship at Cammel Lairds, so he was handier down town. The two unhappy ones were Dad and me. Didn`t we let Mum know! We really gave her a bad time. I was horrible,but to no avail. Back down we went.

The house we moved to was down by the Docks which after living on the Woodchurch was awful. The house had no bathroom and the loo was outside. Even the flats had had a bathroom so now we had to get a bath in the old fashioned tin type. This was hung on a nail on the yard wall, and had to be dragged in and filled with hot water from the kettle or the little electric water heater. With an outside loo to me it was going backwards and primitive so Mum got more bad times. How could she do this to us? Dad worked on the docks and as he said "I don`t want to live by them". So Mum had to suffer for that too.

So Dad along with his fifteen year old daughter thought they had the worst Wife and Mother in the world. The next twelve months were pretty awful for Mum who paid the price for leaving the Woodchurch Estate.

Auntie Kit also wanted to move back down town, so they moved up off Laird St into Plumer St. Again we are all within walking distance of each other. Mum was happy to be close to her Mum but Dad and I were still giving her a hard time.

Dad really hated living there so close to the docks. The biggest reason I think was because of me. There was a road near to where we lived which was well known as a place where the `Ladies of the Night walked` and so sailors from all over the world who didn`t know the area very well would approach the wrong women. So Dad was always worrying when Mum and I were out. As a result I was on a curfew and always had to be home by ten and this lasted until I was eighteen. I hated that walk home because as I got closer to home some of the sailors would jabber in their own language. I never knew what they were saying and sometimes I got really frightened. So if a Docker was going on the night shift I would ask if I could walk with him but when Dad found out he went mad asking how did I know if the Docker could be trusted. As a result from then on he would walk to meet me.

Now You`ve Grown Up Your Future Is Sown Up

Now it`s June 1955. I am fifteen and ready to leave school and the new college in Borough Road opened and Mum and Dad wanted me to take Shorthand and Typing. I wanted none of that so no qualifications meant I had to go into a shop or something similar.

But before I started looking Mum said "As Peggy and Dickie are getting married in August, when you leave school in July you can have the school holidays off" I was going to be one of their bridesmaids.

Here Comes The Bride

August 1955 it's the wedding and our bridesmaids dresses are waiting to be put on,-lovely Lilac in the A line style touching the floor. Susan who was only five wore pink I think, and Peg wore a beautiful long white dress and long veil.

We were taken to Our Lady's Church by black Limousine and it was only the second time I had been in a car. I had been on the back of motorbikes but buses were the usual way of travelling. So now we felt and looked like film stars. All the guests inside waiting for the bride to float down the aisle and she looked beautiful. All the guests in their beautiful new clothes and the ladies wearing fancy hats.

The men in their smart new suits and lovely white carnations in their button holes and the ladies pink carnations were pinned to their dresses. It's August so the weather is warm and everybody is happy. Outside the bride and groom get their photo taken and then it's our turn and finally family and guests. It was magic but more was to come.

The reception was held at Holyoake Hall in Laird St. Auntie Kit and Uncle Fred laid on a lovely buffet for the guests. We had ham salads with trifle for afters. You have to remember food was still not in abundance. Salad was easy to get because of all the allotment growers who were happy to sell salad items but the ham and butter was a different kettle of fish so I wouldn`t be surprised if Auntie Kit hadn`t made one of her journey`s to Ireland to buy the food you couldn`t get here.

The tables had fresh flowers on top of sparkling white sheets used as tablecloths. All the dishes and cutlery were hired from the Hall owned by the Coop and everything was laid out with the help of friends and organised by Auntie Kit who drew on her experience she had had of arranging street Parties. She did a lovely job.

There was no bar in the hall so the beer and bottles of shorts were brought in by the family. Nobody paid anything all day. Maybe some people would go to the pub for a while between food and evening but mostly everyone stayed and nattered. In those days having your weddings planned for you had never been heard of unless you were well off but they could not have had a better time than we had.

Knee`s up Mother Brown

Let the dancing begin. The tables and chairs were pushed to the side so the music and dancing could start. A combo of a piano, drums, banjo and accordion was to provide the entertainment. We didn`t need a singer as we had enough of our own so after the band had warmed up and a couple of drinks had been drunk the party was off.

The performers were ready to perform but the music had moved on a bit so it wasn`t all war songs. We now had singers doing Dean Martin, Frankie Laine and Meryl`s friend sang a Johnny Ray. He was the number one teeny bopper idol who always ended up crying when he sang and our Johnny did it, tears and all. Our Georgie always liked singing so I imagine our Peggy`s wedding was his stage debut. He was a big fan of Mario Lanza a big movie star who was a tenor.

Now we, his sister and two brothers knew he was no Mario because he always sang in the bath albeit at that time it was the tin bath that was carried into the kitchen. Like his snoring he was loud and not beyond getting a boot thrown at him even in the bath but!!!, this was a wedding so we just went out of earshot. Not Mum she stood in front of the stage and proudly declared "That`s my son" we thought she was mad because as I have said her brothers were great singers but it didn`t matter to her, Georgie was great. So did all these insults from his siblings worry our Georgie. Not one bit. He loved to sing, and so sing he did. I have to say that his brothers and sister never got up to sing.

Then the dancing began, and all the adults who had learnt to dance at the Penny Hops showed us kids their expertise and dancing prowess. They could dance the Waltz, the Quick Step, all the Latin American dances, the Rumba, the Cha-cha-cha and my favourite the Samba which had enough rhythm for me to do a type of jiving albeit my type of jive. It was a fantastic time. `Strictly come dancing` had nothing to compare with a wedding in the forties and fifties.

Meryl Hulse, Lolly Casey, Dickie, Peggy, Freddie, Me
(Catherine Wallace), Dickie's niece, Susan Wiggins

The Party's Over

So the wedding was now over and my holiday was coming to an end. Two days later in fact. I was sent off to the Co-op head Office to look for a job. Easy-`Start tomorrow. So I was sent off Derby Rd as an assistant working with two elderly spinsters who obviously didn't like teenagers because the first words were not "hello welcome" but "It's your job to look after the cats". Now I am not a lover of cats so this is not what I want to hear. There were two old smelly cats who right off didn't like me anymore than I liked them. So after a day cleaning shelves and feeding cats for two ladies who never spoke to me all day I decided the co-op wasn't for me. I went home that night and told Mum and Dad I hated it, Dad said "pack it in" Mum said" after you find another job".

We were able to get jobs easily in those days because there was a labour shortage. It was only twelve years after the end of the war and so many people had died and been injured. It meant we could find work and if we didn`t like we left. Not a bit like today where you find a job and have to stick to it pretty much.

The next day was Tuesday and I was at the Grocers with Mum and Mrs Smith the Grocers wife told me that the wholesalers over the road on Conway Street were looking for girls to pack shop orders. There and then Mum frog- marched me over the road and asked the owner for a job for me. Easy again!! "Start tomorrow". So as you can see Mum was never going to let me be out of work.

Tuesday- I started and I liked it, putting orders together for shops to sell. Nothing hard and I made nice friends there. One in particular was Pat Noonan. We were good pals and we walked to work together which took us about twenty minutes and we would see the same people each day. We would say hello and wave.

We had to walk past the Corporation Yard where the dustbin wagons came out every morning. As we passed so the men on the Lorries would whistle. We would wave all in good fun, but then one morning we were late for work and we were running as one lorry came out and the lads shouted for us to jump on the back. There used to be a standing board where the men stood so we stood on with them. It was hilarious, because we used to get a bit dressed up for work and stilettos were the height of fashion so we were in our finery and going to work on the back of a dustcart. It must have made a few people laugh that day.

I made a few friends there. I was to spend the rest of my teenage years with- Jean Quayle, Dot Reid, Edna Jones, Mary Small and her cousin Anne Sheridan. We would go on to have a fantastic time as teenagers. Also I met a girl named Barbara who taught me how to jive. So as `Rock and Roll` came on the scene I could change over easily. I have a lot to be grateful for to her.

I stayed at the wholesalers for about eighteen months and I think I was getting a bit fed up with putting together shop orders. So when there was trouble over the lorry drivers getting a half a crown a week pay rise (which in today's money is twelve and a half pence) and we were getting nothing we, the women, decided to withhold our labour and strike. But the bosses said strike and you are out. So the married ones stayed and the young ones went off.

By the way my pay for working five and a half days eight thirty until five thirty was one pound and seventeen shillings and six pence. In new money that is one pound and eighty seven and a half p. I gave my Mum one pound five shilling for my keep and I had seven and six for me (thirty seven and a half p) in new money.

The next job I went after and I'm sorry to say I got lasted a whole week. It was in Lyons cake factory where I was given a white overall which almost touched the floor, also a Turban which was a white square headscarf and was wrapped around your head. It ended up in a knot on the top of my head to cover my hair which was not at all fashionable so we left most of our hair exposed to look a bit more glamorous which it didn't. It was the same industrial uniform for nearly the whole of women kind. We didn't bother taking them off when we went home so it was nothing to see women dressed in a white overall Coat and Turban on the streets morning and night. So much for hygiene.

My job was to roll up the miniature Swiss rolls that had been covered in jam by hand. There was no machinery to do this so we, the women stood all day rolling while some poor souls further back were smearing the jam on the rolls to send them along to us. As you can imagine when the end of the day came we went home covered from head to foot in jam. So when Thursday came I told Dad I didn't want to stay there and he said "Ok leave!!" but Mum was a different kettle of fish, "You had better find another job quick" she said, so the next day I told Percy the foreman, I was finishing. He offered me a job pouring chocolate onto the Swiss Rolls instead, so the choice was going home covered in jam or chocolate. Bye bye Swiss Rolls.

I think the difference between Dad and Mum was Dad couldn`t say no to his little girl but Mum who had worked at one of the worst jobs you could get thought the ones I was walking away from were OK. So she didn`t like to think I would be out of work. I never was because by Monday I was told Littlewoods Pools were taking on staff.

The other thing that was happening at this time was Mum being not well. She had come out in a dreadful red rash all over her hands and wrists and she couldn`t go to work and when it didn`t clear up after a couple of weeks she was sent to see a Specialist who after many questions decided it was caused by stress. They covered her hands in coal tar bandages which meant she couldn`t do anything around the house and Nan came every day to look after us all.

I think Nan made Dad and I realise we had caused the stress because of the way we had been when we had left the Woodchurch which by now I had pretty much forgotten about. Now, we didn`t like ourselves very much. We made a couple of resolutions for both of us to be nicer and for me to help out more around the house. Dad decided to save up hard and move us out of the house he hated.

For the next two or three years this is what he did and finally Mum`s hands healed. Mum changed her job at Norman Foods and went to work at the Town Hall as a cleaner. She loved this job and took great pride in her work polishing the courts which gleamed and shone.

Her great friend Gertie Houghton worked there too. Mrs Houghton had lived in the flats as well. She was great at sewing on her hand machine. When we were still in the flats, and she was making curtains, she needed two hands to push the material through the needle. She needed help to turn the handle. It was my job to turn the handle-whether I wanted to or not.

She always had a cigarette in her mouth and she never took it out. While I turned the handle I waited for the roll of ash to drop. It never did. It got longer and longer. While she concentrated on a straight seam,I was mesmerized by the roll of ash dangling at a downward angle. Then she would replace it with another cigarette. I never ever saw that ash fall on the curtains, although I wished and wished for it to fall.

By the time I was nineteen Dad kept his promise and moved us to a house on Singleton Avenue in Prenton. Dad was told by the Estate agent that he was the first Docker he knew of who had bought his own house. But that was Dad, determined when he wanted something bad enough. Mum was thrilled with her new house and I think it was a lovely place to live. But that was in the future.

Littlewoods

It was now June 1957 I was almost seventeen and about to start work at the place where I was to spend the rest of my working life and I loved it. The thing about Littlewoods was you either loved it or hated it and if you hated it you left and if you loved it you were there for life. I made so many friends there and still see some of them now but on that first day I met a new friend Heather White. Now this was the place to be. Our wages had tripled, you certainly had to work hard but the money was great.

So we started in the post room Heather and I. We only worked a three day week and got paid for four because it was the summer season. In those days there was no English football in the summer- only Australian football. These were the matches that were used on the coupons and not many English fans were interested in Aussie football so they never sent a coupon in during the summer. However, we didn't know this and consequently we thought this nice easy pace was the norm but come August we would find out differently. So three days on four days off with a bigger pay packet and no jam was paradise! But come August the Post Room became manic now the English football season had begun for real. Down from the pool came trays and trays of postal orders which had to be separated into pigeon holes for the different amounts of money. So as the girls upstairs opened the post, down it came to us, postal orders by the hundreds of thousands. This went on all day Friday and most of Saturday. Paradise Lost.

As the year went by we were sent to training School for the pool where we hoped to end up, where all the coupons were marked. So back to the classroom, not my favourite place but you had to learn all about marking, checking, ordering money to pay out the winners. Now marking was fine, opening post good and I was not bad with most things except ordering money and balancing the order sheet!!! No way could I get a balance. When I had finished training the teacher wished me well but doubted I would ever master ordering and paying out.

We then went onto the Pool as potential Pools clerks and had to sit next to a very experienced pool clerk who had to help finish your training. Each day you could be sitting next to someone different and the first girl they sat me next to was Shirley Houghton from St Andrews Square and I hadn`t seen her since we left. So that was lovely and just further along the row was Sally Millward my cousin and Monica Bastow who eventually became my aunt when she married Mums younger brother, my uncle Peter. They really looked after me and showed me the ropes.

So many of the girls brought up in the flats worked in Littlewoods and it was great to know so many.

Oh No, Not Group One!

Now I am eighteen and time to officially move onto the Pool. Relying on your trainer to help when things went wrong was now all gone and you would be on your own.

One of the things you learnt was you didn`t want to get a position on Group One for three reasons. One was-the supervisor Miss Potter didn`t like teenagers. two, all your post came from

Wales which had addresses in a foreign language – Welsh- which seemed like it to us. The third reason was Army camps- because troops were always on the move and you had to change their Billet addresses as they left the camps and sort out the ones who arrived on the camp. So when you opened post on Saturday and had to sort the coupons to their addresses in a foreign language or change addresses of men who never stayed still for more than six weeks you could get quite a bit behind the other girls whose position was straight forward with normal addresses.

So come the Monday when we were frogmarched onto the pool and I am hoping to get a position close to Shirley or Sally but no such luck. I am sent down away from group ten and ended up by Miss Potter who nodded me towards position twelve. I sat down and looked at the coupons that would be mine to look after and I couldn't believe it, not only did I have a Welsh position but also an army camp in Shrewsbury which bordered Wales, so Bingo!!! I hit the jackpot, Miss Potter, Wales and the army. A nightmare `let me wake up`. There was only one group that had the camps and Wales and only a couple of positions that had both and I got one of them so when the new pool clerks met at dinner time they felt sorry for me, but happy it wasn't them.

After a few months of being one of the last to finish and having also to cope with the ordering and paying out of the winners I finally managed to cope with all the drawbacks of this awful position because the girls around me helped when they could. Also a new building opened in Cardiff and most of the Welsh coupons moved there and life became so good so I could enjoy my job.

In the next batch of trainees I was really happy to see my old pals Edna, Jean, Mary, and Anne who had started and it was great to be back together again. Along with Heather these were to be my pals for all the carefree days ahead.

Oh` Happy days

In Littlewoods there was always someone organising days out with Blackpool being top favourite. We were all teenagers out for a good time and Blackpool was in its heyday. The best form of travel was a coach which had been hired to take about thirty of us. We headed out and sang all the way. Connie Francis songs were great to sing to` Stupid Cupid`, `Lipstick on your collar,`` Ma he`s making eyes at me` and `Who`s sorry now,` We sang at the tops of our voices all the way to wherever we went.

When we went to Blackpool we headed straight for the fairground to the Big Dipper, then the Water Flumes, soaking wet onto the Waltzes, and into the Ghost Train. I was a terrible coward on the Ghost Train because the minute we disappeared through the door I would shut my eyes and scream all the way around and never opened them again until I got off. I never ever saw what was inside the Ghost House but I certainly screamed. My imagination was probably worse than the real thing. Once we had had enough of the fair we would head for something to eat and then pile into a pub where there was a piano and more Connie songs, `You were only fooling while I was falling in love`.

At the end of the day it was time to go home but first we had to round up the incapables and get them on the bus. There was more singing from the girls who hadn`t fallen into a heap and slept all the way home. Mary and I would lead the singing all the way home and laugh when we realised we had walked all the way to Blackpool and back on that bus. By walking I mean always on the move, never sitting down.

1956 and Elvis says
"Let's Rock And Roll"

The biggest music event for the teenagers of the fifties was the Advent of Elvis Presley. Now many teenagers in later years would claim Elvis as their own but he wasn't 'theirs' he was 'Ours, Do you hear, 'Ours'. The first time we heard 'Blue Suede Shoes' and 'Jailhouse Rock' we were blown away. The new American sound and dance 'Rock and Roll' hit England. We had never heard anything like it. We were dancing dances called The Waltz, The Foxtrot, and The Quickstep the dances shown on 'Strictly Come Dancing' today. These have been bopped up a bit but in our day everybody seemed to have a serious face and in the new hip language we were learning 'Square man square'. We didn't mind Latin American because you could do a kind of jive but the new singers coming from America were like nothing we had ever heard.

Paul Anka sang 'Diana' and 'Put your head on my shoulder.' He was only fifteen, Big Bopper sang 'Splish Splash I was taking a Bath' and 'Baby you know what I Like' Bobby Darren sang 'Dream Lover' and probably a favourite of everybody was Buddy Holly who had so many hits I can't pick one out.

The whole teenage population was devastated when a plane carrying Buddy Holly, The Big Bopper, and Frankie Valance came down in a snowstorm and our heros perished

At last teenagers were free, well nearly free as I still had to be in for ten o clock and there was no arguing with Dad.

Hey, Hey, Rock and Roll

So with all the freedom we had, Teenagers were changing in lots of ways. We loved dancing so we loved going into the Ballrooms. The Kingsland and the Tower in New Brighton were top favourites not because we liked the square stuff but for half an hour it was bring on Rock and Roll. When we tried to have a bit of a Jive to maybe a Samba a voice would boom over the mike "No Jiving on the floor please", but when our half hour was announced we would hit that floor and all the `Squares` would hurry off.

We were also choosing our own clothes and that was when the Teddy boys who chose suits they called `The Drape` came into being `The Drape` had a jacket down to their knees with a velvet collar and drainpipe trousers, the narrower in the legs the better, a white shirt and a tie that was like a shoelace. In their top pocket their most prized possession was a comb which they took out all the time to comb their Tony Curtis haircut which was worn sleeked back. It was higher on the top as high as the Brylcream would allow and the sides swept back to meet at the back and the comb would be run down where the sides met into a crease called a DA a (Ducks A!) and that`s why they kept combing to make sure the crease and quiff were always where they should be.

Tony Curtis was a top film star who brought in this style but he didn`t wear it as high as the Teds. It was Elvis who lifted it higher. The Tony Curtis style was adopted by the Mods. It was the shoes that finished off the outfit. It was like Elvis said `You can do anything you want but lay off my blue suede shoes`!! They had very thick soles which added a couple of inches to a lad`s height, and they earned the name of `Beetle Crushers` or Brothel Creepers. When you put them at the bottom of tight drainpipes trousers and a very long jacket you then had every parent`s nightmare. Add their reputation of liking a fight and it was `oh my God don`t bring one of them home here`.

The Teddy Girls wore long black tight skirts with the hem about eight inches above the ankle with white blouses and a black shoelace tie, black cardigan, flat black shoes, and a hair style to match the lads.

The Teds were usually great rock and rollers but there were exceptions to the rule. Our Richie was one of them, God love him he had no sense of rhythm. I had tried to teach him the basics and he did try but he never found the rhythm. As I say he was a Ted and when he went out he took great pride in his appearance. His drape was pressed, his shoes cleaned with the suede brush. He always took ages to get his hair perfect. So with money in his back pocket, comb in his top pocket he hit the Town. The thing about Teds was they loved to bop as we all did but when the Rock and Roll session ended they were never happy about it so they would leave and when they got outside there was usually a fight and the lovely smart drapes and hairstyles were no more. The police were called and our Richie sometimes wasn't quick enough getting away and he was carted off to the Police Station to the horror of Mum but Dad would just go and pick him up, "One day you'll end up in jail and lose your job and then where will you be" our worried Mum would cry but he didn't care, he got a couple fines and a good telling off. He would promise that he would be good, until the next time!! or he went into the Army.

The name of the Teddy boy suits came from the Edwardian era where the gentlemen of the day wore long jackets and tight trousers.

Our Eddie who had just finished National Service was not a Ted. He was the opposite. The soldiers coming back from abroad hadn't heard of `The Teenage Revolution` so when he came back from Hong Kong The

Drape and hairstyle of the fifties Teddy Boys

where he had been for eighteen months he had a great tan and his hair was bleached blonde in the sun. He also had gorgeous silky Italian style suits, Italian shirts with short collars worn with a collar pin and Italian style shoes. This style was just becoming fashionable but the silky material of the suits was still rare.

When he went to the dance at the weekend he cut quite a figure and the girls wondered who this blonde Adonis was. "I`m a pilot" he would say one week or "I`m a Naval captain" the next or maybe SAS another. I remember sitting in work one Monday and Pat the girl sitting behind me was talking about this Test Pilot she had danced with at the Tower the previous Saturday describing his tan and his lovely suits. When I got home I asked "Were you a test pilot last Saturday? He said" yes how did you know," "Because the girls were talking about you at work" but when the tan wore off he had to declare he was a poor student.

I belonged with the groups who dressed the opposite to the Teddy girls. The style we chose were bright coloured blouses with sleeves that were very wide from the neck and tapered to the Cuffs. The skirts were cut out to a full circle worn just below the knee and underneath we wore stiff organza petticoats which made the skirts stand out like a ballerina`s tutu. Not that we danced like ballerinas. Our shoes were the new style. Stilletto`s at least four inches high, but on real special occasions we would wear six inches. But we always had our Flatties in our bags for bopping or walking home when our feet were blistered and sore. Our style was more like the teenagers in the film `Grease`. I am talking about Sandy`s first outfit not the second. `If only`.

Our Georgie was not a Mod or a Ted. He was a Square. He loved the old style dancing, Waltzes and Quicksteps and was still driving us crackers with his singing to his reflection when he was getting ready to go out, but you couldn`t upset him with insults. He completely ignored us. He thought my music was total rubbish, Elvis couldn`t sing a note but I thought the same about his favourites Mario Lanza and Robert Earl to name two, but I must admit I have always enjoyed singing the songs they sang. I don't think our Georgie ever sang to Elvis or Little Richard.

Georgie was the quietest of the four of us apart from his singing. He had a great sense of humour and always seemed to be grinning.

Eddie, Dad, Richie, Georgie

One Two Three O'clock Four O'clock Rock

At this time the record that you couldn't listen to and stay in your seat, was Bill Haley and the Comets playing 'Rock Around The Clock'. You only had to hear the first note and you had to bop. He wasn't gorgeous like Elvis and his music was totally different but he was the one we practised to for hours and hours in somebody's front room.

I remember on my day off from work on a Thursday I was supposed to help Mum around the house and Nan would be there. My job was to clean and polish the front room, so I would put on rock and roll music and before long Bill would have me rocking and my partner would be the door handle and I would be having a really great time, no polishing getting done until Mum could stand the music no longer. "Get out your driving me mad with that noise. Go and see your mates" I never needed telling twice.

Another time when I was about seventeen in 1957, I was in serious trouble when Bill and the Comets came to the Liverpool Odeon and we queued for hours for tickets. I was under strict orders to be in for ten thirty. I was given a whole half hour permit to be late from Dad.

On the night we were all dressed up, over to Liverpool and into the Odeon. The atmosphere was electric and we sat in our seats waiting for that big moment.

Finally the other acts had finished and the manager came out and said "I know you are excited" "We are, we are", "And I know how hard it is waiting for Mr Haley", "We are, we are". He had no idea how hard it was for us while we were waiting. What did he know about excitement? "I want you to promise you will stay in your seats" "We will, we will", "No dancing in the aisles" "We won't, we won't", "Ok then promise" "We do, we do". So off he went, happy in the knowledge that we would behave ourselves!! Then the theatre went into darkness and silence. The place was so quiet you could feel the anticipation, I felt sick with it. Then a loud voice said "Ladies and gentlemen. Then Silence for the build-up. Mr Bill Haley and the Comets" then the music" One two three o clock four o clock Rock" and the place lifted. It was amazing. We stood up and then onto the seats, arms in the air. We were itching to get in the aisles. The Teds who took no notice of the manager ran into the aisles and grabbed the girls and they were away bopping and rocking. We were all so jealous and Bill played on, 'Shake rattle and roll', `Everybody Razzle dazzle` and lastly `See you later alligator`.

After it was all over we dashed outside to see if he would come out on the Roof. "We want Bill, We want Bill". We chanted for about half an hour but he didn't come out. But the night was not over. I looked at my watch it was after ten and I was still in Liverpool. There was no way I could get home for ten thirty. We all started running and got on the train. I was in trouble. When I got close to home I could see Dad waiting in the place he always met me. The dreaded look and "Get up those stairs I'll sort you out tomorrow". I can't remember what tomorrow brought but seeing Bill Haley probably made it all worthwhile.

Even up to a few years ago I loved to dance to Bill. But where I once prayed for his music to be played now I pray it isn't. The mind is willing but the flesh is weak. 'See you later Alligator' became the way we teenagers said bye to each other and the reply was 'In a while Crocodile'. We were real hep cats.

Bill Haley and Elvis

We`ll join the Army and see the World!
OK! Well what about Italy

At the time when we were all eighteen in 1958, we decided we would like to join the Army and see a bit of the world. So off we went to the recruitment office. Apart from me there was Mary, Jean, Edna, Anne, and another girl who`s name I can`t remember who thought it was a good idea to go with us. We got the forms to take home to be signed by our Dads whose permission we needed because we were not yet twenty one although lads were called up for the Army at eighteen to fight.

I put the forms on the table in front of Dad. He took one look and said "You are not going". When we arrived at work the next day only one of us had permission. That was the girl who`s name I can`t remember and off she went on her own.

Our next adventure was to be a holiday in Italy. On the pool there were three girls who were older than us. They were in their early twenties and didn`t need a signature from their father to travel. We thought these girls were the height of sophistication. They were going on holidays to very exotic places so we wanted to be as sophisticated and go to exotic places too. We all started to save and pretty soon we had enough money, about thirty five pounds we needed.

Off we went to the travel agents to book a holiday. We felt very grown up when we said we wanted a holiday in Italy and out came the brochures then the booking form. "Take the form and get your parents to sign it then come back and pay your deposit then off you can go" said the agent. We looked at each other. Nobody can object to a holiday can they!!! So off we went home. I put my form on the table in front of Dad. Again he took one look at it and said "You are not going" and so again when I got into work nobody was going. Sophistication went out the door.

That was how it was for most girls then. Parents worried when their daughters wanted to go off by themselves and we accepted it. We have certainly come a long way since then so I suppose it was my generation of women who decided the girls of today could look after themselves as well as any lad and now they trot off all over the globe. Good Luck girls I say.

Margaret, Heather, Me and Dot

Time passes very quickly when you are having a great time. Fridays and Monday we went to the Cinema to see the latest films and favourite heart throbs. My favourite at this time was Marlon Brando- very handsome with dark brooding eyes. On Thursday we went to the Carlton pub for a sing song and a drink, then on to the Kingsland for the half an hour Rock and Roll session, then back to the Carlton for another sing song. The best night was Saturday when we went to the Tower in New Brighton and a sing song at the Perch Pub which was always full of your mates from Littlewoods.

Dad was easing up and letting me come in later but I always had to be on the last train from New Brighton unless Edna or Heather had gotten off with a lad with a car. There weren't many lads with cars then so the lads who had a car had the pick of the crop. So Edna and Heather who could pick and choose too, chose lads with cars. We others would wait outside and wait for the girls to say "You don't mind giving my friends a lift do you" and most didn't but some told us to get lost and then we had to run for the train but we would laugh all the way home.

Let It Snow, Let It Snow, Let It Snow

The New Year of 1958 I was allowed a special pass by Mum and Dad. This was probably because they were going to a party themselves and didn't know what time they would get home.

After a great New Year's Eve night in the Tower we came out knowing that we would have to walk home because all the buses and trains had finished. While we had been dancing the night away the snow had been coming down and there was a thick layer everywhere. We had to walk home from New Brighton. There were hundreds of us, everybody in a happy mood after singing Auld Lang Syne. If you were on your own it didn't matter you- just tagged on.

The girls had changed into their flatties for the long walk and pretty soon the snow was scooped up and snowballs were flying everywhere. It was fantastic, everybody ended up soaked but happy. We went the rest of the way singing and laughing. One time we had been invited to a party in Birkenhead and when we had walked down Gorsey Lane into Duke Street we spotted a Taxi. We asked him to take us near the Town Hall. He said he was going home but it wasn't far from where he lived and he would take us. We piled in and headed off down Conway Street and when we got to the Art School the Taxi broke down. It wouldn't start and the driver asked us to push, we did. It still didn't start so we pushed again and again until we finally gave up at the Ritz. The driver thanked us and we felt so sorry he wouldn't be able to work the next day we insisted on paying our fare. How stupidly generous were we. The driver must have thought it was Christmas all over again.

Now I am eighteen and Dad has kept his promise to move us out of Massey Street and we moved into Singleton Avenue. Mum was very happy to be there- so was Dad and I loved it. The lads weren't that bothered and Georgie now had a bathroom to sing in, and we couldn't get in there either. Eddie was at University in

Liverpool and Richie was still in the Army Stationed in Germany and didn't get home much.

The first thing I did was buy a bike to get to work and I loved riding up and down Borough Road and past the Library where I had gone to with my cousins Margaret and Barbara when we visited Uncle Albert and Auntie Annie. They lived just over the road from the Library and they were another family I thought were well off because they went upstairs to bed. But I couldn't stop and visit because their little two up and two down had been pulled down and is now a- wait for its a Carpark! They had moved onto the Woodchurch as we had moved off.

Sentimental Journey

So as I draw to a close, the story of my childhood and teenage years, I have to admit that they were very good years. Although we were war babies we were to have wonderful times. As children we weren't deprived of very much, food was scarce but the ones that really went without were our parents.

We were surrounded by relatives, friends and neighbours for years because people lived in the same neighbourhood for years and looked after each other. The older people were cared for even by their neighbours. When I came home from school I would have to go to the shops and Mum would always say "See if Mrs Godfrey or Mr Griffiths wants anything before you go," They were our elderly neighbours. Mrs Godfrey was a great cake maker and although she was elderly she still made little sponge fairy cakes and I was always rewarded with one. Mr Griffiths tried to give me a copper but no way was I allowed to take money.

Also if any woman was scrubbing her step she made sure she did the step for anyone who couldn't. The front step and brasses were the pride and joy of the women in those days.

Now when I think back to those days, I remember everyone, school friends and all the kids I played with in the flats, and pals on the Woodchurch Estate, it makes me very nostalgic. Aunties, Uncles , cousins and the really close ones, Nan, Auntie Kit and Uncle Fred, our Peggie who took me everywhere she went, and the only price I had to pay was to brush her hair until it shone. She was the big sister I didn't have.

Sadly we drift apart and only get together when someone is ill or dies as was the case when Auntie Kit died and at the Funeral Dad and Uncle Fred were the last two of our lovely Parents. They had been very close pals for sixty odd years and were sitting quietly remembering their youth.

The Bike Ride

Today Auntie Kittie was buried, Our Parents are disappearing fast. The two patriarchs are holding court. Dad and Uncle Fred, the only two left,

Auntie Kit's husband and brother going over old times

"Remember, George, when we went to Llandudno on our bikes?"

"Aye I do Fred. The weather was good and no punctures"

We stand around in a semi circle, daughters, sons, nieces, and nephews. We know we are about to hear of one of their days out they spent together in their poor but happy youth. These two great pals of sixty years and more.

"And do you remember that nice old lady we went to for a drop of water for a cup of tea"

Dad nodded slowly remembering. "And she asked how far we had come and when we told her she said we must be hungry and could we eat a bit of bacon and egg"

"Yes, and when it came it was bacon, egg, sausage, black pudding and tomato"

119

Uncle Fred took to thinking.

"You are wrong there George there wasn't any tomato"

"OH There was! There was bacon, egg, sausage, black pudding and tomato I can see it on the plate"

"You can't see tomato"

"I can see it and I can taste it.

"Well your memory is letting you down, Bacon, egg, sausage and black pudding was all that was on the plate"

"Fred you've forgotten the tomato"

By this time the listeners are getting restless and I say "Does it matter if there was or wasn't any tomato on the plate. Does it have any relevance to the story"? Dad gave me a cold look.

"When you suffer through a depression, when you can't get work, when you get hungry and the best meal you are likely to get is blindy,*and when someone puts a feast in front of you, you don't forget if there is tomato on the plate, and I don't know if it has any relevance to the story because I have forgotten what the bloody story is.

That was Dad and Uncle Fred, always quietly happy in each other's company.

*Blindy. Fried onions, sliced potato, gravy salt simmered in a shallow pan in a tiny drop of water, also called Blind Scouse and very tasty. It was named Blindy as there was no meat in it.

Dad and Uncle Fred

Mum, Nan and Dad

I remember Mum and Dad were always chunnering away at each other which I suppose is what most married couples do. They had been married fifty four years when Mum died. They had kept us entertained for years when they started having a go at each other, always ready with a reply. But no matter how often they argued they never used bad language or shouted at one another, but they were certainly worth listening to. After I was married I loved to listen to them at their best.

What Do You Want From Me Pet?

One day while visiting my parents
My father he put on his cap
My mum she looked at him slowly and said
"Where are you going in that?"
"I thought I would go for a walk" said Dad
"Well isn`t that typical of you

Every day you go missing, leaving me it all to do
Dad replied "Don`t worry Pet
If you want, I`ll stay in and help"
"Don`t you go to no trouble now, I`m used to doing it myself
Dad he looked at Mum and thought
"Is she ready to have a go
I`ll have to choose my words carefully
I`ve got to confuse her I know.
Now these conflicts came up quite often
As a rule Dad didn`t say much
I could see today would be different
So I told the kids to hush.
"If I stay in I never go out
If I go out I never stay in.
And when I do the sweeping
I do a lousy job,
If I never offer
I`m just a lazy slob
Should I get the ladders out to give the glass a shine
You say it`s inconvenient
Do them some other time.
"Tell me Susie Sweetheart?
What do you want from me?
I want to make you a cuppa! But!!
I make a lousy cup of tea"
Mum she stood there speechless.
Then I began to laugh.
I never knew her stuck for words,
How would she give it back
    But
She turned her head towards me
And she began to smile
I knew I was the target
Nowhere could I hide
She curled her top lip upward

My face began to flush
I knew that you`d stick up for him,
Cos your tarred with the same sodden brush.

The Wiggins and the Kellys, families, cousins and friends. We always seemed to be together. Mum and Auntie Kit, Dad and Uncle Fred always within walking distance. We celebrated together and were sad together. I couldn`t have chosen a nicer Aunt and Uncle, and cousins- especially our Peg. She took me with her when she went to the shops and to see her friends and never let me feel a pest.

When she was a teenager she still never chased me away. What I remember most was the clothes she bought. When she was fed up with them she let Auntie Kit cut them down into outfits for me, so I was lucky enough to be quite well dressed.

And lastly my Nan, my lovely Nan. I never saw her angry even when times were hard and always the peace maker if anyone was arguing. When I think of her and put a picture in my head I always see her at her kitchen sink, up to her eyes in soap suds, and the floor swimming with water. She would be wringing out the sheets which would curl round and round her arm like a giant snake and always her tongue would stick out, pressing hard against her top lip with sheer exertion. When she finally got a mangle I would love to turn the handle while she pushed the washing between the rollers and the water was squeezed out. Then we had a lovely cup of Connie Onnie tea in a jam jar when we had finished.

When she finally was left on her own all of her family wanted her living with them. After I married she came on holiday with us and we loved having her with us.

Finally

    To my children and grandchildren this little offering I hope will show you how we lived and played through the War Years. We sang through the forties and into the fifties and bopped as teenagers. We loved being young as all youngsters should.

       They are after all the best years of our lives.

Are You One of Us

From the family names of Kelly, Downey and Wiggins we will have amassed hundreds of cousins all over the world and I hope that maybe one of you one day will be interested enough to follow your other side of your family.

My Research

When I first set foot inside St Werburg's Church to look at the records I didn't think I was setting out on a hunt for my ancestors that would take me seventeen years. That I would go to Ireland many times and fall in love with the country and people. I have met relatives I didn't know existed. A friend I have known since we were seventeen turned out to be a cousin as both our Granddads were brothers. These kinds of revelations and coincidences happened a lot and were fantastic when they happened.

So what did I discover?

The Kellys

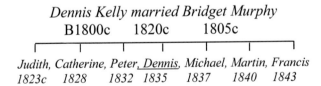

Dennis Kelly married Bridget Murphy
B1800c   1820c   1805c

Judith, Catherine, Peter, Dennis, Michael, Martin, Francis
1823c   1828   1832 1835   1837   1840   1843

Back in 1835/circa Dennis Kelly Junior, was born in a very small village named Boherbaun between Monastrevin and Athy in Co Kildare Ireland. The family were poor as were most of the Catholic population at that time. They rented their own small plot of land in which to cut peat on Monvullagh Bog. They lived in the tiny hamlet of Cloney Bridge.

Dennis senior married Bridget Murphy in the Catholic parish church of St Mary`s in Monastrevin. They had seven children that I know of. I found Peter, Dennis, Michael and Martin in the church records as well as the 1861 Birkenhead Census. I was then able to trace them as witnesses in marriages and as godparents to the children of the brothers.

I also found a strong link to a Joseph and Michael Lawler who are very possibly cousins but that's another story.

The four brothers left Ireland 1858-59. At least two of the brothers settled in Birkenhead, Peter and Dennis.
Peter married Elizabeth Dempsey.

Catherine Ralston, my great Grandmother, was the Granddaughter of Ellen and John Coghlan.

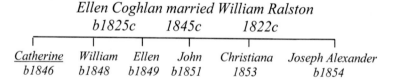

Ellen? married John Coghlan
b1787   Cork   b1780c

Ellen Coghlan married William Ralston
b1825c   1845c   1822c

Catherine	William	Ellen	John	Christiana	Joseph Alexander
b1846	b1848	b1849	b1851	1853	b1854

Both of Catherine`s parents died young. Her Mother Ellen died of typhus when she was thirty one. The children were looked after by their Grandmother Ellen Coghlan. She was a widow and a midwife.

William Ralston was born in Belshills, Lanarkshire, Scotland. There are no clues as to who William might be apart from being a Stonemason and working on the Statue of Liberty. He died in America of heatstroke at the young age of twenty nine.

Dennis and Catherine married in St Werburghs Church, Grange
Road, Birkenhead. .

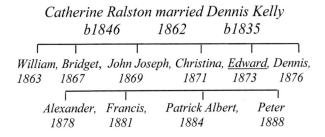

Catherine Ralston married Dennis Kelly
b1846   1862   b1835

William,	Bridget,	John Joseph,	Christina,	*Edward*,	Dennis,
1863	*1867*	*1869*	*1871*	*1873*	*1876*

Alexander,	Francis,	Patrick Albert,	Peter
1878	*1881*	*1884*	*1888*

Catherine Kelly nee Ralston,
Bridget, Patrick, and a
grandchild(?) Feala.

Catherine with children,
Christina, John Joseph,
Edward, William and Dennis

127

*Patrick Albert and
Brother Edward*

<u>Edward Kelly</u> married <u>Margaret Mooney</u>
1895
My Grandparents

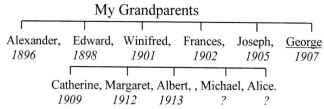

Alexander, Edward, Winifred, Frances, Joseph, <u>George</u>
1896   1898   1901   1902   1905   1907

Catherine, Margaret, Albert, , Michael, Alice.
1909   1912   1913   ?   ?

George married Susan Downey the daughter of Susan and Richard Downey and they had four children George, Edward, Richard and me Irene.

Catherine (our Kit) married Frederick Wiggins. They had five children. Freddie, Margaret (Peggy), Mike, Francis, and Susan.